The Idiot's Guide To
CHILDREN'S PARTY CAKES

ANN PICKARD

MEREHURST

ACKNOWLEDGEMENTS

My special thanks to Vicky Hillman and Fiona Cowling for their help in preparing this book, and, as always, to my friends and family.

Also to J. F. Renshaw, Crown Street, Liverpool L8 7RF (tel. 0151-706 8200), for supplying the sugarpaste used throughout.

The Publisher would like to thank the following suppliers:

**Anniversary House
(Cake Decorations) Ltd**
Unit 16
Elliott Road,
West Howe Industrial Estate,
Bournemouth, BH11 8LZ

Guy, Paul and Co. Ltd
Unit B4
Foundry Way,
Little End Road,
Eaton Socon,
Cambs., PE19 3JH

Cake Art Ltd
Venture Way
Crown Estate,
Priorswood,
Taunton, TA2 8DE

Squires Kitchen
Squires House
3 Waverley Lane,
Farnham,
Surrey, GU9 8BB

Published in 1995 by Merehurst Limited
Ferry House, 51–57 Lacy Road, Putney, London SW15 1PR
Cake designs and text Copyright © Ann Pickard 1995
Photography and design Copyright © Merehurst Limited 1995
ISBN 1 85391 462 2

A catalogue record for this book is available from the British Library.

Managing editor: Barbara Croxford
Editor: Helen Southall
Designer: Anita Ruddell
Photographer: James Duncan

Colour separation by P&W Graphics Pte Ltd
Printed in Italy by Canale & C SPA.

CONTENTS

THE CAKES

INTRODUCTION

THIS BOOK IS A SIMPLE AND EFFECTIVE GUIDE to creating a variety of children's party cakes using the minimum of equipment and time.

All the cakes in this book are Madeira sponges coated in sugarpaste and decorated with sugarpaste models. Clear instructions for coating a cake in sugarpaste are given on page 8; read this and the section on making models (pages 12–15) before you start to make a cake. Following instructions carefully is the key to achieving perfect results.

THE BASICS

The following is a brief guide to the essentials needed to prepare and coat your cake ready for the models to be assembled:

The Cake

A recipe for Madeira sponge is given on page 6. The sizes and dimensions you require for each cake are given at the beginning of each design.

The Cake Filling

For extra flavour, slice cakes horizontally in half and sandwich back together with layers of jam and filling cream (see page 6).

Sugarpaste

Sometimes referred to as 'fondant' or 'roll-out' icing, and easily bought in supermarkets and sugarcraft shops, sugarpaste is available in many different colours. Using ready-coloured paste can save a lot of time, especially with darker colours, such as red, green and black.

Apricot Glaze

This is used to secure sugarpaste to cake boards, and can also be helpful when making models (see page 13). A simple recipe is given on page 6.

Royal Icing

This is used for piping grass and hair, or creating a 'sea' effect. A recipe is given on page 6.

The Cake Board

Always use cake 'drums' (in preference to thin cake cards or boards) as these will support the weight of the finished cake without bending. This is especially important if the cake is more than 25cm (10 inches) across.

Tips

☆ Always use a cake board that is at least 5cm (2 inches) wider than the cake.

☆ Old, marked cake boards can be used again if you cover them with icing.

☆ Do not always place the cake in the centre of the cake board; a design is more interesting if the cake is offset on the board.

COLOURING SUGARPASTE

If you cannot buy ready-coloured sugarpaste in the colour you require, buy white sugarpaste and colour it yourself. Use paste colours for best results as they are more concentrated and give deeper, richer colours. The basic colours you will need are: yellow, red, dark blue, turquoise, pink, green, chestnut brown, orange and black. To make some colours, you will need to mix together some of the basic colours: for purple/lilac, mix pink and blue; for a dull leaf green, mix green and brown; for 'flesh', mix tiny amounts of pink and yellow; for peach, mix pink and yellow; for grey, use a very little black colouring; for sand, mix orange, yellow and brown; for 'teddy bear' colour, mix orange and brown.

The Basic Colours

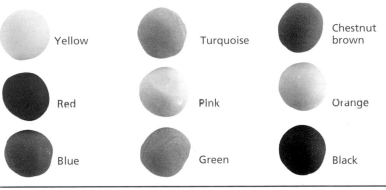

Yellow

Turquoise

Chestnut brown

Red

Pink

Orange

Blue

Green

Black

Mixed Colours

Purple/lilac: pink and blue

'Flesh': pink and yellow (tiny amounts of each)

Grey: a tiny amount of black

Sand: orange, yellow and brown

Dull leaf green: green and brown

Peach: pink and yellow

Teddy: orange and brown

To colour sugarpaste, follow these simple steps:

1 Make a hole with your thumb in the middle of the piece of paste to be coloured. Dip a cocktail stick (toothpick) into the colour, then put the colour into the hole.

2 Fold the paste over and start to knead the colour in, using icing (confectioner's) sugar to prevent it sticking to the work surface or to your hands. Add more colour as necessary to achieve the colour you require, but take care not to add too much.

Creating a Marbled Effect

1 Divide the sugarpaste (white or cream) in half and add colour to one half until it is a slightly darker colour than you require.

2 Add the remaining white or cream sugarpaste and knead lightly together. Roll out to create a marbled effect.

BASIC RECIPES

APRICOT GLAZE

THIS MAKES A USEFUL 'GLUE' for sticking sugarpaste to cake boards, and for sticking parts of sugarpaste models together (see page 13). Simply brush it on with a fine paintbrush; the water added to the jam should prevent the glaze setting as it cools.

- 3 tablespoons apricot jam
- 1 teaspoon water

Put the jam and water in a small saucepan and heat gently until the jam melts and boils. Tip into a sieve set over a small bowl and rub the jam through the sieve with the back of a spoon.

FILLING CREAM

- 125g (4oz) margarine or butter, softened
- 185–250g (6–8oz/1–1½ cups) icing (confectioner's) sugar, sifted
- 1–2 tablespoons water
- vanilla essence

Put all the ingredients together in a bowl and beat until a light, fluffy consistency is achieved.

ROYAL ICING

- 90ml (3fl oz) albumen solution (reconstituted egg white) or pure egg white
- 500g (1lb/3 cups) icing (confectioner's) sugar, sifted
- 1 teaspoon glycerine (glycerol)

Put all the ingredients together in a bowl and beat with an electric mixer on slow speed until a peaked consistency is achieved.

MADEIRA SPONGE

A MADEIRA SPONGE BASE is recommended as it will keep moist and fresh for several days if wrapped in foil and stored in an airtight container prior to decorating. Madeira sponge is also less crumbly than a Victoria sandwich or whisked sponge.

1 Preheat the oven to 180°C (350°F/Gas 4). Grease the required tin and line it with greaseproof or non-stick paper.

2 Put the butter, margarine and sugar in a bowl and cream together until pale and fluffy.

3 Add one third of the eggs and one third of the flour and gradually beat in. Slowly add the remaining egg and flour, one third at a time. Finally, fold in the lemon zest, if using.

4 Turn the mixture into the prepared tin and bake in the oven for the time given in the chart, or until a fine skewer inserted in the centre comes out clean. Leave to cool in the tin.

Tips

☆ Always store royal icing with a damp cloth over it.

☆ A tiny speck of blue colour can be added to make your icing look whiter.

Madeira Sponge Ingredients Chart

	20cm (8 inch) round or oval	20cm (8 inch) square	25cm (10 inch) square
butter, softened	90g (3oz)	125g (4oz)	185g (6oz)
margarine	90g (3oz)	125g (4oz)	185g (6oz)
caster (superfine) sugar	185g (6oz/¾ cup)	250g (8oz/1¼ cups)	375g (12oz/1½ cups)
eggs (size 3, medium)	3	4	6
self-raising flour	155g (5oz/1¼ cups)	185g (6oz/1½ cups)	280g (9oz/2¼ cups)
plain flour	60g (2oz/½ cup)	90g (3oz/¾ cup)	140g (4½oz/1¼ cups)
grated lemon zest (optional)	1 lemon	1 lemon	1 lemon
baking time	40–50 minutes	50 minutes to 1 hour 10 minutes	1 hour 10 minutes to 1 hour 25 minutes

EQUIPMENT

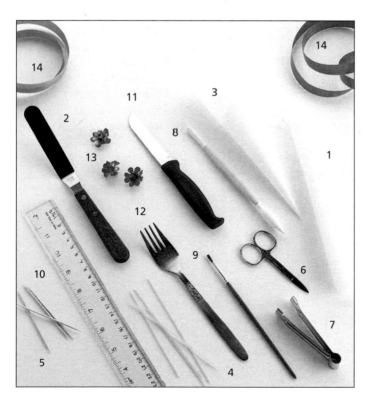

THE CAKES IN THIS BOOK can be made using basic equipment. The following is a list of the most useful items.

1   Small non-stick rolling pin
2   Small 'elbow' (cranked) palette knife
3   Greaseproof or non-stick paper for piping bags
4   Raw dried spaghetti
5   Cocktail sticks (toothpicks)
6   Small sharp scissors
7   Crimper
8   Impressing tool (such as a PME Tool no. 9, which is round at one end and pointed at the other)
9   Paintbrush
10 Ruler/tape measure
11 Sharp kitchen knife
12 Fork
13 Silk flowers
14 Ribbons

PREPARING AND COATING CAKES

PREPARATION

To prevent the cake base from crumbling while being shaped and decorated, bake it a few days in advance of the party, allow to cool and then freeze it. When you are ready to decorate it, remove it from the freezer and allow it to thaw slightly. While the cake is still partially frozen, cut the square or round into the desired shape. Turn the cake upside-down (so the flat base is now the top) and stick it to the cake board with a smear of filling cream (see page 6).

Slice the cake horizontally in half and spread jam and filling cream on the bottom half. Replace the top and if the surface of the sponge is uneven, use a large serrated knife to skim off the top surface and make the cake perfectly flat. Spread a thin layer of filling cream all over the cake with a palette knife. The cake should still be frozen enough to stop the surface crumbling. Leave the cake to thaw completely (1–3 hours) before covering with sugarpaste. (If you coat the cake with sugarpaste before it has finished thawing, the surface of the paste will become wet and sticky.)

COATING WITH SUGARPASTE

As the initial coating of sugarpaste forms the basis for the decoration, try to achieve as smooth a finish as possible. Follow these simple steps:

1 Roll out the recommended amount of paste in the chosen colour, using icing (confectioner's) sugar to dust the rolling surface. The rolled-out sugarpaste should be 4–5mm (about ¼ inch) thick.

2 Using a ruler or tape measure, check that the paste is rolled out to a large enough area before picking it up to place it over the cake: For a 20cm (8 inch)

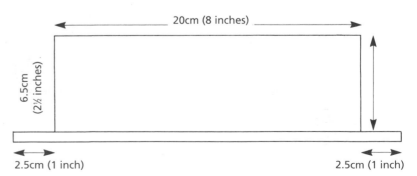

20cm (8 inches)

6.5cm (2½ inches)

2.5cm (1 inch)   2.5cm (1 inch)

square cake that is 6.5cm (2½ inches) high, you will need to roll out the paste to a 33cm (13 inch) square (20cm/8 inches + 6.5cm/2½ inches + 6.5cm/2½ inches = 33cm/13 inches). If you wish to cover the board around the base of the cake as well, roll out the paste so that it is 5cm (2 inches) larger (38cm/15 inches square for a 20cm/8 inch square cake).

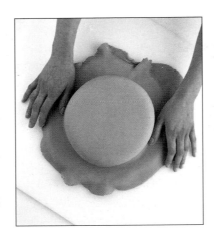

3 Place the cake as near as possible to the piece of rolled-out paste. Either pick up the paste by hand and drape it gently over the cake, or wrap the paste around the rolling pin, pick it up, lift it over the cake, then unroll the sugarpaste over the cake.

4 At this stage, do not press the paste against the base edge of the cake. Instead, start from the top edge and gently smooth the sugarpaste

down the cake sides with the palms of your hands, working your way around the cake and gradually moving lower. When you get to the base of the cake, press the paste in firmly all around the base, and trim off excess neatly.

5 If you are coating the board as well, when you have completed smoothing the paste all around the cake, cut off the excess neatly around the edge of the

<table>
</table>

Tips

☆ To coat the cake board in advance instead of at the same time as the cake, roll out some sugarpaste until it is 4–5mm (about ¼ inch) thick and slightly larger than the board. Spread a thin layer of apricot glaze on the board, lift the paste on the rolling pin and unroll it on to the board. Press down firmly and trim off excess. Air bubbles can be removed by pricking with a cocktail stick (toothpick) and smoothing over with your hand.

board. Immediately lift the edges of the paste and brush a little apricot glaze underneath. Press the paste firmly down on the board all around the cake. Ensure no jam seeps out from underneath and shows. If this does happen, wipe it away with a clean, dry tissue or cloth (a damp one will mark the sugarpaste).

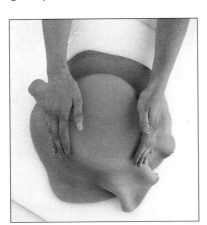

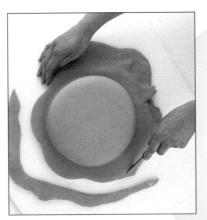

FINISHING TOUCHES

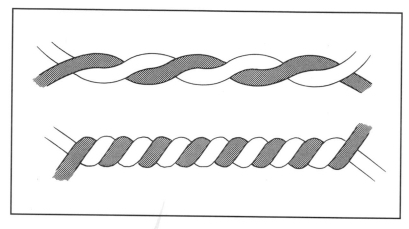

Once the cake and board are covered, the edges of the sugarpaste can be finished in a number of decorative ways while the paste is still soft; a 'rope' or embossed roll of paste looks attractive around the base of the cake. Frilling techniques can also be used to great effect.

Rope

Roll out two sausages of sugarpaste about 5mm (¼ inch) in diameter as long as possible and of equal length. Brush off excess icing (confectioner's) sugar and place the sausages side by side on the work surface. Starting from the centre, twist them around each other, working in both directions at the same time. Place the 'rope' around the base of the cake. Try to arrange pieces of 'rope' so that any joins are at the back or corners of the cake.

'Ropes' can be made from two different colours of sugarpaste, or all the same colour for a more subtle effect. Squash the pieces very slightly against the cake to secure.

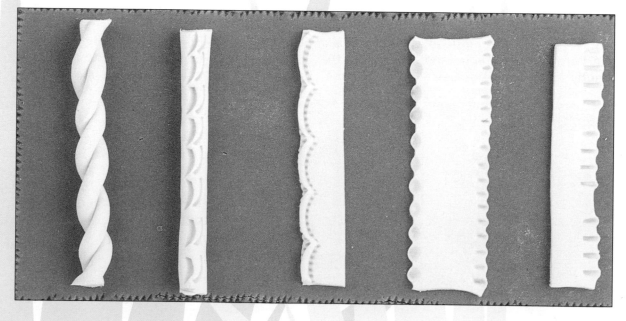

Roll

Roll out a sausage of paste about 5mm (¼ inch) in diameter and as long as possible. Brush off any excess icing (confectioner's) sugar and place the paste around the base of the cake, squashing very slightly to secure. Use the edge of a modelling tool to press a decorative pattern in the roll all around the cake, or use crimpers to crimp a pattern. Press the crimpers into the sugarpaste roll, squeeze them together, then release and open them while pulling away. Repeat all around the cake.

Crimped Edge

To crimp the edge of the sugarpaste to give a decorative finish around cake or board, place the edge between the teeth of the crimpers and squeeze the crimpers together. Release and open the crimpers as you pull them away. Repeat all around the cake.

Tooled Edge

Use a pointed or ball modelling tool to mark a decorative pattern all around the sugarpaste edge. The handle of a teaspoon can also be used to great effect (see The Mouse's Tail cake on page 57).

CREATING A FRILLED EFFECT

A frilled decoration can be made by cutting strips of sugarpaste and frilling them. Pressing quite firmly, roll a cocktail stick (toothpick), the end of a paintbrush handle or a pointed 'frilling' tool along the edge of the paste until it stretches and frills. Attach frilled strips to cake or board, ensuring that the joins are at the corners of the cake or cake board.

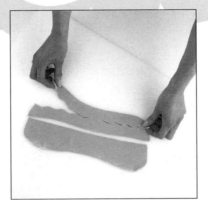

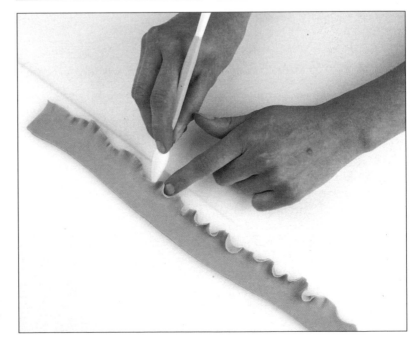

MODELLING IN SUGARPASTE

THE MODELLED ANIMALS and figures that appear in this book are what give each cake its individual charm and character. They are not difficult to make once you have mastered the basic technique.

1 To start making a model, such as the simple pig illustrated right (which is an easy model to practise on), either use ready-coloured sugarpaste or colour the appropriate amounts as required. Each cake design gives details about the total amount of paste needed and about how much should be coloured in the different colours used, if necessary. The pig is simple because all the sugarpaste required is coloured pink.

2 Place all the sugarpaste in a polythene bag to prevent a skin forming. (If making a model in several colours, put the different-coloured batches of paste in separate bags.) To shape the first part of the model (the pig's feet, for example), pull a piece of paste out of the bag and shape it into the size of ball required according to the instructions given and following the 'Guide to Sizes' below. For the pig's feet, you would need to mould the first piece of paste into four size F balls.

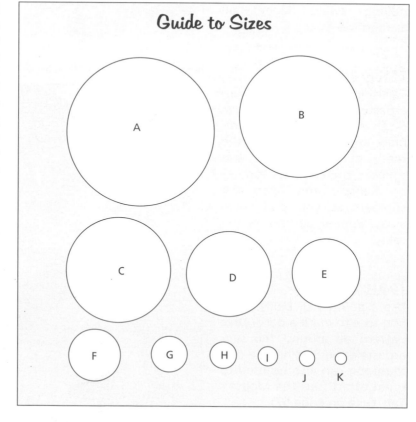

Guide to Sizes

A B C D E F G H I J K

3 Roll each piece of paste in turn into a smooth ball between the palms of your hands; the warmth of your hands will soften the paste and remove any lines or cracks from its surface. Once formed into a ball, check that it matches the size given in the guide. Add or take away paste and reroll the ball as necessary until it matches the size given in the chart. Return excess paste to the polythene bag.

4 Shape and position the first piece of the model as required, then take more paste out of the bag to make the second, and so on until the model is complete. Repeat to make more models the same, if required; do not attempt to make more than one at a time. It is a good idea to practise making models before you start making a cake. Full instructions for making the pig are given on pages 16–17.

Full instructions for making the pig are given on pages 16–17.

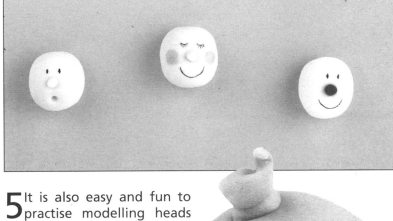

5 It is also easy and fun to practise modelling heads from smooth balls of paste, adding different features and expressions. Noses are easily made from tiny balls of paste, while eyes and mouths can be painted on or marked with a pointed tool.

Tips

☆ It is important to work with only one small piece of sugarpaste at a time when making the models, and to keep any paste you are not using in a polythene bag. If sugarpaste is left exposed to the air it will form a skin which will make it impossible to stick the pieces together. Colour the sugarpaste first, put it in a bag, and pull out pieces, one at a time, for shaping into balls as required.

☆ If you find the warmth of your hands is not sufficient to make pieces of paste stick together when making a model, use a little apricot glaze brushed on with a paintbrush. It is also possible to buy edible 'gum glue' which can be used to help secure pieces of sugarpaste together or to attach decorations to cakes.

MODELLING IN SUGARPASTE ☆ **13**

PIPED DETAILS

A very little simple piping is required to finish off some of the cake designs in this book. For example, the hair on the Rag Doll (see page 29) and some of the other figures is piped on, as is the green ivy on the Haunted House (see page 35). However, this piping work is very easy and is mostly achieved using only paper piping bags without the need for piping tubes (tips). Coloured royal icing is used for this. Make up a quantity following the recipe on page 6 and colour small amounts with tiny dots of paste food colouring.

Making a Paper Piping Bag

1 Use non-stick (silicone) or good-quality greaseproof paper. Cut a 30cm (12 inch) square and cut it in half to form two triangles. Hold one

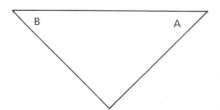

triangle in front of you with the top point towards you and the longest side furthest from you.

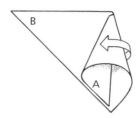

2 Curl the right-hand point (A) inwards to meet the point nearest to you and to form a cone shape with its tip halfway along the longest side of the triangle.

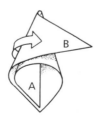

3 Holding the two points together firmly, fold the remaining point (B) round the outside of the cone and bring it down to meet the other two points. Pull the

three points together firmly so that a sharp point is formed at the tip of the cone. Continue pulling point B around to make the cone as tight and narrow as possible.

4 To prevent the bag unravelling when you put it down, fold all the points inwards.

Tip

☆ Before filling a paper piping bag with icing, make sure it is formed into a good point. If the paper begins to unravel, the hole in the tip will get bigger, and the icing will flow straight through! Secure the bag firmly, following the instructions in steps 3 and 4.

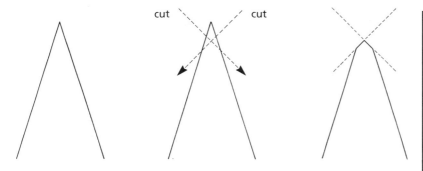

cut   cut

Piping Hair and Grass

1 Fill a small paper piping bag half full with royal icing (coloured as required), and cut the tip of the bag off at an angle with two snips of the scissors, as shown in the illustrations above.

2 Touch the tip of the bag to the model's head, or to the surface of the cake or board, and squeeze out a small blob of icing. Stop squeezing, and pull the tip away, drawing the icing into a point.

3 For short, spiky hair and grass, pull the tip of the bag away sharply, leaving just a short 'spike' of icing. For longer 'blades' of grass, pull the tip of the bag away more gently, drawing the icing out into a longer point. Repeat until you have piped enough hair or grass.

Piping 'Permed' Hair

1 Fill a small paper piping bag half full with coloured royal icing, and squeeze the

icing down towards the tip of the bag. Pinch the tip of the bag flat and snip off 2–3mm (about ⅛ inch).

2 Touch the tip of the bag to the figure's head and start to squeeze icing out of the bag. Continue to squeeze as you gently pull the tip away from the head, allowing the icing to fall in a long strand or 'ringlet'. When the 'ringlet' of hair is long enough, stop squeezing and pull the tip of the bag away. Repeat until you have piped enough 'ringlets' to cover the figure's head.

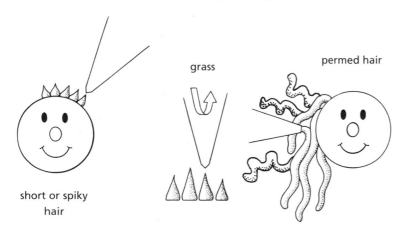

short or spiky hair

grass

permed hair

PIGS IN A FARMYARD

PROBABLY THE EASIEST CAKE DESIGN in this book, and pigs are surely the most popular of farmyard animals – a winning combination!

You will need

- 18cm (7 inch) square cake
- 25cm (10 inch) square cake board
- jam for filling
- filling cream (see page 6)
- 1.1kg (2lb 2oz) white sugarpaste
- brown, pink and black food colourings
- icing (confectioner's) sugar for dusting
- apricot glaze (see page 6)
- impressing tool
- 60g (2oz) royal icing (see page 6)
- 375g (12oz) sugarpaste for pigs
- cocktail stick (toothpick)
- bite-size Shredded Wheat
- ribbon to trim board

PREPARING CAKE AND BOARD

1 Place the cake on the cake board. Cut the cake horizontally in half and fill with jam and filling cream.

2 Divide 1.1kg (2lb 2oz) sugarpaste in half and colour one half dark brown. Add the remaining white paste and knead together lightly to create a marbled effect (see page 5). Roll out the paste and use to cover the cake and board together, following

Size Guide for Pigs
(see page 12)

	large pig	piglet
feet	4 x F	4 x G
body	A + D (rolled together)	C
head	C	E
snout	E	G
ears	2 x G	2 x H
tail	H	I

☆ Remember! Roll and shape each ball of paste as you need it, not in advance.

the instructions on page 8. Scratch the surface in places with the pointed end of an impressing tool to give the 'farmyard' a more realistic, rough surface.

3 Colour the royal icing a 'muddy' brown colour and smear at random with a palette knife on to the cake and board to represent mud.

PIGS

4 Colour all the sugarpaste pink and put it in a polythene bag. Start by making one large pig, followed by three piglets. All the pigs are made in the same way.

5 For the feet, roll four balls between the palms of your hands and arrange them

7 For the ears, squash the two balls of paste flat and pinch one side into a point. Push the rounded ends of the ears into the head, points upwards. Bend the tip of each ear downwards towards the nose. Mark the eyes with the tip of a cocktail stick (tooth-pick) dipped in black food colouring.

8 For the tail, roll the ball of paste into a sausage shape with a point at one end. Make a small hole in the tail end of the pig and push the flat end of the tail into it. Twist the tail around until it forms a curl. Leave to harden.

FINISHING

9 Place the pigs in position on top of the cake and on the board, securing them with some royal icing 'mud'.

10 Arrange some bite-size Shredded Wheat around the pigs on the cake and board to represent bales of straw and a pig sty. Trim the cake board with ribbon.

in a square with equal space between them. Make up a ball of paste for the body, mould it into an oval shape and place it on top of the feet. Press down firmly. Mark 'toes' on the feet with the pointed tool or a cocktail stick (toothpick).

6 For the head, make an indentation with your finger in one end of the body and press the ball of paste into it. Place the snout in position, flattening the ball of paste slightly as you press it on. Mark two big nostrils in the snout with the pointed tool.

TEDDY IN A BOOT

THIS CHARMING TEDDY will appeal to the very young. For older children, the boot could be changed into a trainer or hiking boot and stood on a grassy base.

You will need

- 315g (10oz) cream sugarpaste for board
- icing (confectioner's) sugar for dusting
- 30cm (12 inch) hexagonal or round cake board
- apricot glaze (see page 6)
- impressing tool
- 20cm (8 inch) square cake, 4cm (1½ inches) deep
- jam for filling
- filling cream (see page 6)
- 10cm (4 inch) round cake, 5cm (2 inches) deep (see Tip, page 21)
- 1.25kg (2½lb) white sugarpaste for 'boot'
- brown, orange, black and green food colourings
- craft knife or scalpel
- 7.5cm (3 inch) plain round cutter
- red paper ribbon
- 175g (6oz) sugarpaste for teddy
- paintbrush
- cocktail stick (toothpick)
- 60g (2oz) royal icing (see page 6)
- small paper piping bag (see page 14)
- silk or sugar flowers
- cardboard gift tag
- ribbon to trim board

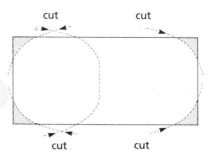

PREPARING CAKE AND BOARD

1 Roll out the cream sugarpaste and use to cover the cake board, following the instructions on page 9. Mark the edges with a decorative border using the impressing tool, and scratch the surface

Size Guide for Teddy
(see page 12)

body	2 x A
arms	2 x D
head	A
ears	2 x G
nose	J

☆ Remember! Roll and shape each ball of paste as you need it, not in advance.

lightly in places with the pointed end of the tool. Leave to harden overnight.

2 Cut the 20cm (8 inch) square sponge into two rectangles measuring 10 x 20cm (4 x 8 inches). Spread one rectangle with jam and filling cream, and place the second rectangle on top. Using a sharp knife, cut off all the corners to give a more rounded shape (see diagram). Place on the covered board.

3 Place the round cake on top of the rectangular sponges, positioning it towards one end and spreading a little jam and filling cream under the round cake.

4 Colour the white sugarpaste mid-brown and shape a small piece into a size B ball (see page 12). Roll the ball into a sausage 10cm (4 inches) long and position it along the join between the top of the rectangular sponges and the bottom edge of the round sponge. Shape the 'sausage' so it curves round the base of the top sponge. Spread all surfaces of the sponge and the sugarpaste 'sausage' with filling cream.

5 Roll out 125g (4oz) of the remaining mid-brown sugarpaste to 5mm (¼ inch) thick. Trace the outline on page 63 on to greaseproof or non-stick paper and cut it out to make a paper template. Lay the paper on the sugarpaste and cut round the template with a craft knife or scalpel.

6 Lay the sugarpaste shape on top of the boot and down the front. Lay the

paper template on top of the sugarpaste on the boot.

7 Roll out another 1kg (2lb) brown sugarpaste to 5mm (¼ inch) thick, and lay it over the top of the cake, smoothing it carefully into place.

THE BOOT

8 Using a plain round cutter or knife, cut a 7.5cm (3 inch) circle out of the brown sugarpaste on top of the cake (revealing the paper template beneath). Starting at the centre of the front edge, make a 10cm (4 inch) cut in the sugarpaste in a straight line down the front of the boot towards the toe. Remove the paper template and pinch the edges of the sugarpaste between your fingertips all around the hole and down both sides of the cut.

9 Using the pointed tool, press six lace holes in the sugarpaste down each side of

the cut. Scratch some irregular lines on the surface of the boot with the tip of the pointed tool to create a worn effect. Mark 'seams' in the boot with a knife.

THE LACES

10 Insert the laces while the sugarpaste is still soft. Cut some red paper ribbon into strips 4cm (1½ inches) long and 5mm (¼ inch) wide, and press the ends of each into opposite holes across the central line. Cut two longer strips of ribbon to make the untied laces at the top.

TEDDY

11 Colour all the sugarpaste 'teddy-bear' colour (see page 5) and put it in a polythene bag. For the body, roll two size A balls between the palms of your hands, then knead and roll them together into one smooth, round ball. Place the ball inside the top of the boot.

12 For the arms, make two size D balls, and flatten each into a long 'teardrop' shape, flattening the fatter ends slightly to represent paws. Fix the narrow end of each arm to the upper part of the body, with the paws hanging over the edge of the boot. Press to stick, brushing on a tiny amount of apricot glaze with a fine paintbrush, if necessary, to help secure them if the warmth of your hands is not sufficient to make them stick.

13 To shape the head, roll another size A ball into a fat teardrop shape, pinching the tip upwards slightly to shape the nose. Use the pointed tool to mark an indentation in the teddy's face for the nose. For the tip of the nose, colour a size J ball a darker brown, roll it

until it is slightly pointed at one end, and press it into the hole at the tip of the nose.

14 For the ears, use a pointed tool to make a 5mm (¼ inch) hole in each side of the top of the head. Squash two size G balls

of sugarpaste flat, and pinch one side of each to a point between your fingertips. Press the points of the ears into the holes, using the pointed tool. Mark eyes and eyebrows with the tip of a cocktail stick (toothpick) dipped in black colouring.

FINISHING

15 Colour the remaining sugarpaste a darker

brown and roll it into a very long, thin sausage. Stick it all around the base of the cake to represent the sole of the boot, using a little apricot glaze to keep it in place.

16 Decorate the board around the boot with piped grass (see page 15) and silk or sugar flowers. Attach a cardboard gift tag to the end of a lace. Trim the cake board with ribbon.

FLYING HIGH

THIS FANTASY CAKE is really up in the clouds! Suitable for father or son, it would also delight grandad!

You will need

- 20cm (8 inch) petal-shaped cake
- 25cm (10 inch) square cake board
- jam for filling
- filling cream (see page 6)
- 1.1kg (2¼lb) white sugarpaste for cake and board
- blue, brown, green, yellow, pink and black food colourings
- icing (confectioner's) sugar for dusting
- apricot glaze (see page 6)
- white ribbon to trim cake
- 250g (8oz) royal icing (see page 6)
- 250g (8oz) sugarpaste for the 'plane and pilot
- sharp knife or scalpel
- raw dried spaghetti
- paintbrush
- impressing tool
- black icing pen
- cocktail stick (toothpick)
- small paper piping bag (see page 14)
- large cloth piping bag
- large star piping tube (tip)
- ribbon to trim board

PREPARING CAKE AND BOARD

1 Place the cake on the cake board. Cut the cake horizontally in half and fill with jam and filling cream.

Colour and Size Guide for the 'Plane
(see pages 5 and 12)

wings (brown)	A
fuselage (brown)	A + C (rolled together)
tail (brown)	E, G (two pieces)
cockpit (black)	F
cockpit rest (brown)	G
nose (brown)	G, H, I (three pieces)

2 Colour 1.1kg (2¼ lb) sugarpaste sky blue, roll it out and use it to cover the cake and board together, following the instructions on page 8.

3 Attach a length of white ribbon around the base of the cake, securing with a dot of royal icing.

THE 'PLANE

4 You will need about 155g (5oz) sugarpaste to make the 'plane. Colour about 15g (½oz) black and the remainder brown. Put in separate polythene bags.

Colour and Size Guide for the Pilot
(see pages 5 and 12)

body (green)	D
arms (green)	F
hands ('flesh')	2 x J
head ('flesh')	E
nose ('flesh')	K

☆ Remember! Roll and shape each ball of paste as you need it, not in advance.

5 Trace the wing outline on page 63 on to greaseproof or non-stick paper and cut it out. Roll a size A ball of brown paste between the palms of your hands, then roll it out to a strip 16cm (6½ inches) long and 2.5cm (1 inch) wide. Lay the template on top and cut the sugarpaste round it with a sharp knife or scalpel. Place the sugarpaste strip on top of the cake.

6 For the fuselage, roll together a size A and a size C ball of brown paste

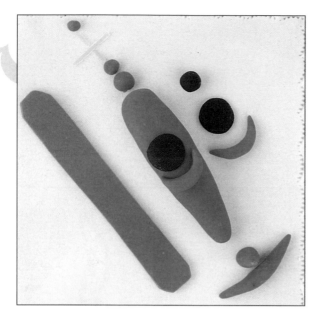

and form into a sausage shape 10cm (4 inches) long. Thin one end to form the tail. Place across the wings on top of the cake.

7 For the tail, roll a size E ball into a sausage shape 5cm (2 inches) long. Taper both ends and position it across the tail end of the fuselage. Mould a size G ball into a teardrop shape and position it on top of the first piece, pointing upwards.

8 For the 'plane cockpit, roll a size F ball of black paste and squash it into a round disc. Press it on to the middle of the fuselage. For the rest behind the cockpit, roll a brown size G ball into a sausage shape 2.5cm (1 inch)

long, taper the ends and position it around the back of the cockpit.

9 For the nose, press a size G ball of paste on to the front of the fuselage, flattening it as you do so. Cut a piece of spaghetti 2cm (¾ inch) long and place it across the nose, pushing it into the sugarpaste. Cut two more pieces of spaghetti, each 5mm (¼ inch) long, and position them at right angles on either side of the first piece. Press a size H ball of paste, then a size I ball, on to the nose, ensuring that the spaghetti pieces stay in place.

THE PILOT

10 Use the remaining 90g (3oz) sugarpaste to make the pilot. Separate out enough sugarpaste for the body and arms and colour it green (or any other colour), then colour the remainder a 'flesh' colour using tiny amounts of pink and yellow colouring. Put the green amd 'flesh'-coloured sugarpaste in separate polythene bags.

11 Form a size D ball of green sugarpaste into a cone shape and place it on the cockpit for the pilot's body. Cut a piece of spaghetti 5cm (2 inches) long and push it down through the centre of the body, allowing the end to protrude at the top.

12 For the pilot's arms, roll a size F ball of green paste into a sausage shape 2.5cm (1 inch) long and taper the ends. Cut the sausage in half and attach one half on either side of the body, pressing the tapered ends to the 'shoulders' of the pilot. Shape the arms round the pilot's body to the front. If necessary, use a little apricot glaze brushed on with a paintbrush to keep the arms in place.

13 For the hands, shape each ball into a teardrop shape. Twist the pointed end of an impressing tool into the end of each of the pilot's arms to make a small hole. Place the pointed ends of the 'hands' into the holes, pressing in well.

14 Roll a size E ball of sugarpaste for the head and make it as smooth as possible. Press it down on to the spaghetti protruding from the top of the body. Make a small hole in the centre of the face with the pointed tool. Mould a size K ball of 'flesh'-coloured paste into a teardrop shape, and push it gently into the hole for the nose. Mark eyes and a smile with a black icing pen or with a cocktail stick (toothpick) dipped in black colouring.

15 Colour some royal icing pale brown and use to pipe hair on to the pilot's head, following the instructions on page 15.

FINISHING

16 Fill a large cloth piping bag fitted with a large star cream piping tube (tip) with the remaining white royal icing, and pipe big fluffy clouds on to the cake and board.

17 Mark flying birds on the sides of the cake and the board with a black icing pen or with a paintbrush dipped in diluted black colouring. Trim the cake board with ribbon in the usual way.

WHALE IN THE OCEAN

YOU'LL HAVE A WHALE OF A TIME making this one! The whale can easily be changed into an octopus or shark by varying the colour and shape!

You will need

- 20cm (8 inch) hexagonal cake
- 30cm (12 inch) square cake board
- jam for filling
- filling cream (see page 6)
- 1.4kg (2¾lb) white sugarpaste for cake and board
- icing (confectioner's) sugar for dusting
- apricot glaze (see page 6)
- impressing tool or cocktail stick (toothpick)
- 750g (1½lb) royal icing (see page 6)
- blue, pink, turquoise and black food colourings
- 185g (6oz) block of white sugarpaste for icebergs
- 185g (6oz) sugarpaste for the whale
- ribbon to trim board

PREPARING CAKE AND BOARD

1 Place the cake on the cake board. Cut the cake horizontally in half and fill with jam and filling cream.

2 Roll out 1.4kg (2¾lb) white sugarpaste and use it to cover the top and three sides of the cake, and the front section of the board, following the instructions on page 8.

Colour and Size Guide for the Whale
(see pages 5 and 12)

body (purple)	3 x A
eyes (white)	2 x I
pupils (black)	2 x K
tail (purple)	C

☆ Remember! Roll and shape each ball of paste as you need it, not in advance.

Use a cocktail stick (toothpick) or the pointed end of an impressing tool to scratch lines in places on the sugarpaste surface.

3 Beat the royal icing until it stands in peaks. Separate half the icing into another bowl and colour it deep turquoise. Add the white icing and fold lightly together until only half mixed.

4 Spread the royal icing generously over the top and sides of the cake, and over the uncovered board, pulling it into rough peaks as you spread it. Leave the front section of the cake and the covered board exposed. Reserve a little of the icing.

5 Cut a 185g (6oz) block of white sugarpaste into jagged pieces and press into the icing on top of the cake to represent icebergs.

THE WHALE

6 Set aside enough sugarpaste for the whale's eyes and colour the remainder purple using pink and blue colourings. Colour about a quarter of the paste for the eyes black. Put the paste in polythene bags.

Colouring Tip

☆ If you have some ready-coloured black sugarpaste, use this for the whale's pupils as it is hard to achieve a dense black with food colouring.

7 For the whale's body, roll three size A balls of purple paste together until smoothly joined. Shape into a teardrop shape, place on a work surface or board, and flatten the pointed end slightly.

8 To make eyes, flatten two size I balls of white paste into ovals. Flatten two size K balls of black paste and press on towards one end of each oval. Press on to the whale's head. Mark a big smile on the whale with a knife. Place the whale on top of the cake, pressing it down into the 'sea' of royal icing.

9 For the whale's tail, form a size C ball of paste into an oval shape and taper the ends. Cut one end in half from the tip to halfway down the length of the oval piece. Open up the pieces and twist them both inwards. Squash each tail fin flat, and pinch the ends to points. Mark lines on the tail with the pointed tool or a cocktail stick (toothpick). Press the tail into the royal icing on top of the cake with the fins pointing upwards.

FINISHING

10 Spoon the reserved royal icing into the gap between the whale's body and tail, and around the sides of the whale. Trim the board with ribbon.

RAG DOLL

THE IDEA OF MAKING A CAKE look like a cushion is very popular and could also be used for a Christening cake. For a more elaborate finish, 'weave' strips of paper ribbon in and out of the cushion following the instructions for the laces on the Teddy in a Boot cake (see page 20).

You will need

- 1.8kg (3lb 10oz) white sugarpaste
- green, pink, yellow, brown, black, red and orange food colourings
- icing (confectioner's) sugar for dusting
- 36cm (14 inch) square cake board
- apricot glaze (see page 6)
- crimper
- impressing tool
- 20cm (8 inch) square cake, 5cm (2 inches) deep
- jam for filling
- filling cream (see page 6)
- 500g (1lb) sugarpaste for rag doll
- raw dried spaghetti
- sharp knife or scalpel
- cocktail stick (toothpick)
- paintbrush
- 60g (2oz) royal icing (see page 6)
- small paper piping bag (see page 14)
- black icing pen
- paper ribbon
- ribbon to trim board

Colour and Size Guide for the Rag Doll
(see pages 5 and 12)

legs ('flesh')	B
shoes (brown)	2 x E
body ('flesh')	A
dress (green)	C
arms ('flesh')	D
sleeves (green)	2 x F
head ('flesh')	D
nose ('flesh')	J

☆ Remember! Roll and shape each ball of paste as you need it, not in advance.

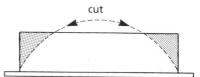
cut

PREPARING CAKE AND BOARD

1 Colour 500g (1lb) sugarpaste pale green, roll it out and use to cover the cake board, following the instructions on page 9. Using a crimper and the ball end of an impressing tool, make a decorative pattern around the edges of the paste. Leave overnight.

2 To give the cake a sloping top, use a large, sharp knife to remove wedges of sponge all round the top (see diagram). Cut the cake horizontally in half and fill with jam and filling cream. Place the cake on the cake board, positioning it close to one corner (see photo opposite).

3 Roll out 875g (1¾lb) white sugarpaste and use to cover the cake following the instructions on page 8. Reserve the trimmings. Mark diagonal lines with a knife in both directions across the cake to create diamond shapes. To give a 'quilted' effect, press the pointed end of the impressing tool into the sugarpaste in the corners of the diamonds.

FRILLING

4 To make the frilled edge of the 'cushion', roll out some of the remaining white sugarpaste about 2.5mm (⅛ inch) thick, and cut into strips 2.5cm (1 inch) wide. Roll a

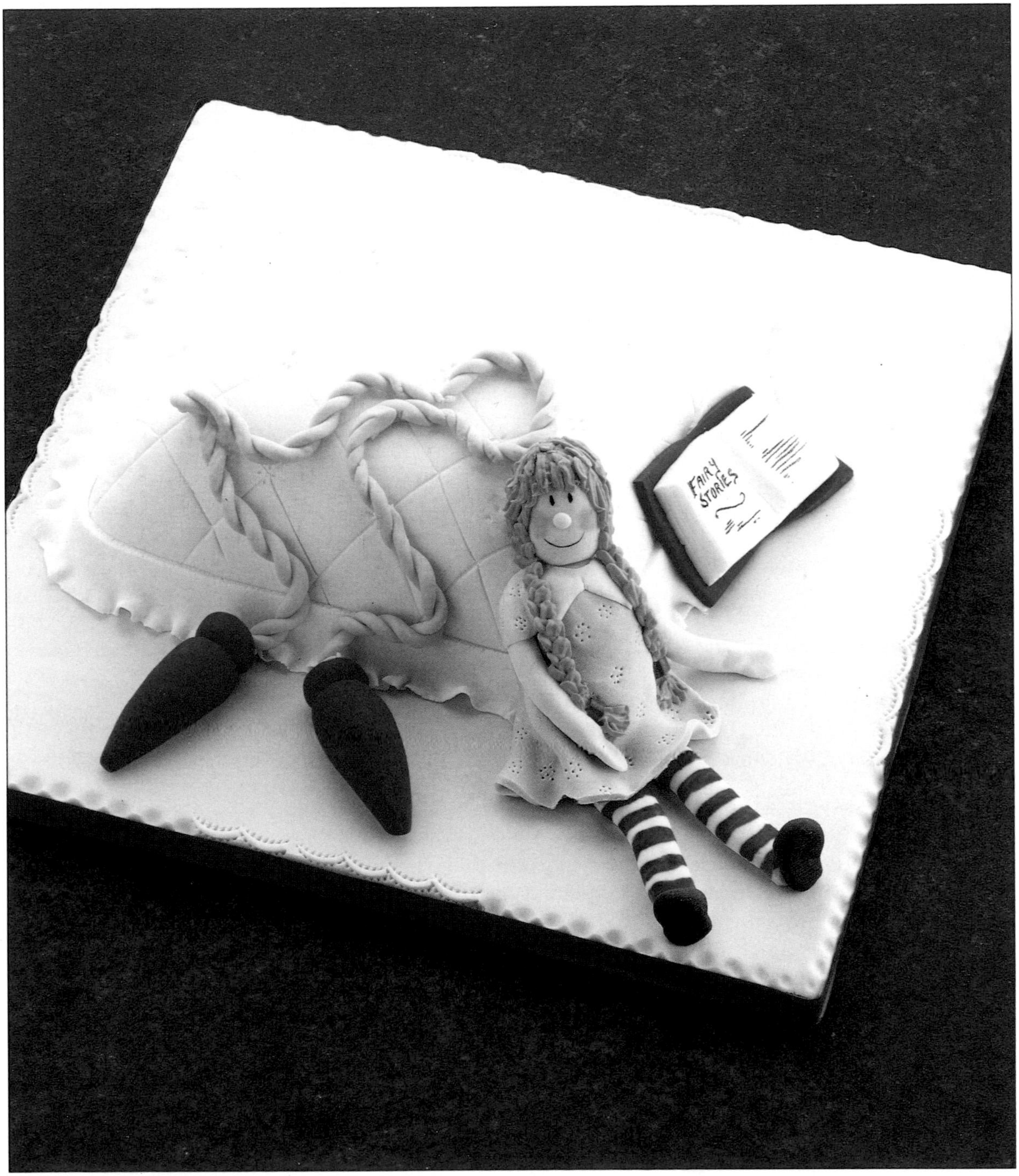
FAIRY
STORIES

pointed tool along the edge of one strip until it frills (see page 11). Repeat to make enough frilled strips to fit all around the cake. Attach the strips to the base of the cushion with a little royal icing or apricot glaze, trying to ensure that the joins are at the corners.

THE DOLL

5 Following the guide on page 28, divide 500g (1lb) sugarpaste into roughly the proportions required for each colour, and colour them as indicated. Place in separate polythene bags.

6 Beginning with the doll's legs, roll a size B ball of 'flesh'-coloured paste between the palms of your hands, and shape it into a sausage 15cm (6 inches) long. Cut the piece in half and place the two pieces side by side on the board at the corner of the cake. Roll two size E balls of brown paste for the doll's shoes, and mould them into slightly squashed pear shapes, pinching them in the centre to shape them. Press them on to the rounded ends of the legs with the widest parts pointing upwards.

7 For the doll's body (under her dress), shape a size A ball of 'flesh'-coloured paste into a cone 5cm (2 inches)

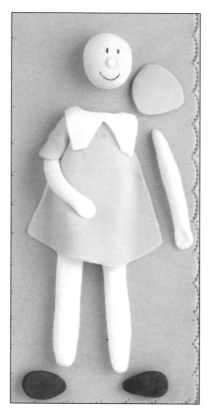

high, and stand it on the ends of the legs, allowing the 'body' to lean back against the cushion. Push a piece of spaghetti down into the centre of the body and break it off, leaving 2cm (¾ inch) protruding at the top of the body.

8 For the doll's dress, form a size C ball of green paste and roll it out thinly. Trace the outline on page 63 on to greaseproof or non-stick paper and cut it out to make a template. Lay the paper template on the sugarpaste and cut out the sugarpaste

round it with a sharp knife or scalpel. Wrap the dress around the 'body', tucking the edges in behind. For the collar, trace the outline on page 63 and cut it out. Roll out a little white sugarpaste and use the paper template to cut out a collar. Attach it to the top of the dress.

9 For the doll's arms, roll a size D ball of 'flesh'-coloured paste into a sausage 10cm (4 inches) long and cut it in half. Flatten the rounded end of each piece for the doll's hands. Taper the other end of each arm slightly and attach to either side of the body. To make the sleeves, flatten two size F balls of green paste and wrap one around the top of each arm.

10 Form a size D ball of sugarpaste for the head and roll it as smooth as possible. Press it down on to the spaghetti protruding from the top of the body. Make a hole in the centre of the face with a pointed tool. Mould a size J ball of paste for the nose and pinch one side into a point. Press it firmly into the hole in the face.

11 Mark eyes with the tip of a cocktail stick (toothpick) dipped in black food colouring, and paint on a smile with a fine paintbrush and diluted black colouring. Paint on rosy cheeks with pale pink colouring.

12 Colour the royal icing yellow and use to pipe the hair and long plaits, following the instructions on page 15. To achieve a plaited effect, pipe the icing in long strokes that cross over one another. Leave to dry.

THE BOOK

13 Cut a wedge of white sugarpaste 8mm (⅓ inch) thick from a block and trim to measure 7.5 x 4cm (3 x 1½ inches). Cut a piece of red paste that is slightly larger and fix the white paste on top of the red with a little royal icing or apricot glaze. Mark firmly down the centre and in fine lines along the sides to give the appearance of pages of a book.

14 Write a message (such as 'Happy Birthday' or '4 today') on the book with a black icing pen or with a fine paintbrush and black colouring. Alternatively, mark black lines across the pages to look like lines of print.

THE SKIPPING ROPE

15 Colour 60g (2oz) sugarpaste a sandy colour (see page 5) and divide in two. Roll each piece into a very long sausage and twist them around one another to form a rope (see page 10). Arrange on the cake with the ends resting on the board. Use a little royal icing or apricot glaze to hold the rope in place, if necessary.

16 For the rope ends, colour 60g (2oz) sugarpaste red. Make two size B balls (see page 12) and shape into long teardrop shapes. Squash a smaller size E ball of red paste on to the fat end of each. Push a pointed tool down into the centre of the fat end of each piece to form a deep hole. Place on the cake board and push the ends of the skipping rope into the holes in the handles.

FINISHING

17 Place the book in position beside the cushion, securing with a little royal icing or apricot glaze.

18 Use a cocktail stick (toothpick) to mark a fine, decorative pattern on the doll's dress. Paint red striped 'stockings' on to the doll's legs with a fine paintbrush and red colouring. Attach small pieces of paper ribbon to the ends of the doll's plaits. Trim the cake board with ribbon.

TRUNDLING TRUCKS

UP AND OVER THE HILL! These little trucks could be loaded with small sweets, or you could push candles into them.

You will need

- cake baked in a 2 litre (3 pint) pudding basin (measuring 20cm/ 8 inches at its widest and 10cm/4 inches high), see Tip
- jam for filling
- filling cream (see page 6)
- apricot glaze (see page 6)
- 28cm (11 inch) round cake board
- 1.25kg (2½lb) sugarpaste for cake and board
- black, green, yellow, orange and blue food colourings
- icing (confectioner's) sugar for dusting
- impressing tool or cocktail stick (toothpick)
- 280g (9oz) sugarpaste for trucks
- paintbrush
- chocolate matchsticks
- 60g (2oz) royal icing (see page 6)
- small paper piping bag (see page 14)
- ribbon to trim board

PREPARING CAKE AND BOARD

1 Turn the cake out of the pudding basin, cut it horizontally in half and fill with jam and filling cream. Spread a little apricot glaze on the cake board and place the cake on the board, position-

(see page 12)

Size Guide for Trucks
(see page 12)

main body	A
cab	D
tyres (black)	4 x G
hub caps	4 x J

☆ Remember! Roll and shape each ball of paste as you need it, not in advance.

ing it towards one side (the back). Spread filling cream all over the cake.

2 Colour 250g (8oz) sugarpaste pale grey with a little black colouring, and roll it out on a surface lightly dusted with icing (confectioner's) sugar. Cut a strip measuring 5–6cm (2–2½ inches) wide and 30cm (12 inches) long (reserve the trimmings). Lay the strip over the centre of the cake to form the road, stretching it down on to the board. Use the pointed end of an impressing tool or a cocktail stick (toothpick) and your fingertips to mark

scratches and indentations in the road surface.

3 Divide 1kg (2lb) sugarpaste in half and colour one half dark green. Add to the other half and knead together lightly, creating a marbled effect (see page 5). Roll out the paste to a 33cm (13 inch) circle and cut it in half across the centre. Use the two pieces to cover the cake and board on either side of the road. (Don't worry about any bumps!)

THE TRUCKS

4 Colour about 15g (½oz) sugarpaste black. Divide the remainder into three and colour each portion a different colour. Put in separate

Tip

☆ To make a cake of the correct size, you will need the same quantity of mixture as for a 20cm (8 inch) round tin (see page 7).

polythene bags. All the trucks are made in the same way.

5 For the main body of each truck, roll a size A ball of coloured sugarpaste between the palms of your hands, and shape into a rounded rectangular shape. For the cab, shape a size D ball of paste into a rounded rectangle. Press the cabs on to the main bodies.

6 Roll four black size G balls for the tyres, flatten them

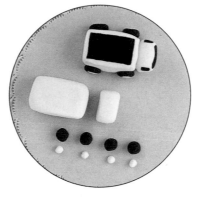

into round discs and squash a small hub cap on to each one. Position on each truck, pressing to secure. Using diluted black food colouring and a

paintbrush, paint in windows and a black rectangle on top of each truck.

FINISHING

7 Use the reserved grey sugarpaste trimmings to make boulders and small pebbles. Place some pebbles on top of each truck.

8 Make a fence on either side of the road by pushing chocolate matchsticks into the sugarpaste. Pile more chocolate sticks on the board at the bottom of the hill to represent a pile of logs. Arrange piles of 'boulders' on the cake and board.

9 Colour the royal icing green and use to pipe 'grass' around the 'boulders' and on the roadside 'verges', following the instructions on page 15. Trim the cake board with a length of ribbon.

HAUNTED HOUSE

THIS SPOOKY CAKE is ideal for any child who wants to combine a birthday party with Hallowe'en, or whose party has a ghostly theme at any time of year.

You will need

- 625g (1¼ lb) black sugarpaste
- icing (confectioner's) sugar for dusting
- 36cm (14 inch) square cake board
- apricot glaze (see page 6)
- crimper
- 25cm (10 inch) square cake
- jam for filling
- filling cream (see page 6)
- 1.8kg (3lb 10oz) white sugarpaste
- pink, blue, green and black (optional) food colourings
- paintbrush
- 185g (6oz) sugarpaste for ghosts
- 2 small paper piping bags (see page 14)
- 125g (4oz) royal icing (see page 6)
- ribbon to trim board

Colour and Size Guide for Ghosts
(see pages 5 and 12)

'body' (white)	A + C (rolled together)
eyes (black)	2 x J
mouth (black)	H

☆ Remember! Roll and shape each ball of paste as you need it, not in advance.

3 Place the house-shaped cake on the covered board and very carefully cut the cake horizontally in half. Fill with jam and filling cream. Place piece A in position for the doorway.

4 Colour 1.5kg (3lb) white sugarpaste pale purple using pink and blue colouring. Roll out the paste and use it to cover the cake, following the instructions on page 8. Mark a brick design in the paste with the back of a knife, and crimp a decorative border around the top edge. Using another 250g (8oz) purple paste, make a

diagram. Remove all the shaded areas, reserving the piece marked A. Slice piece A horizontally in half and discard one half.

PREPARING CAKE AND BOARD

1 Roll out 500g (1lb) black sugarpaste and use to cover the cake board following the instructions on page 9. Using a crimper, mark a decorative border in the sugarpaste around the edge of the board. Leave to set overnight.

2 To make the shape of the house, cut pieces out of the cake as illustrated in the

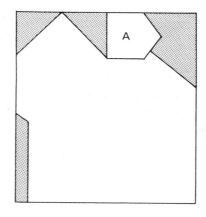

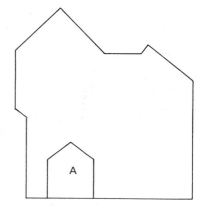

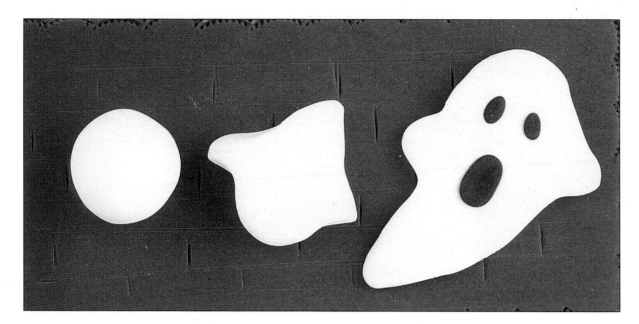

'rope' to place around the base of the cake (see page 10).

WINDOWS AND ROOVES

5 Trace the window and roof outlines on page 64 on to greaseproof or non-stick paper and cut them out. Roll out 125g (4oz) black sugarpaste and use the paper templates to cut out two large and three small windows, two roof pieces for the top of the house, and one smaller roof piece for the doorway. Crimp the front edges of the roof pieces. Brush any loose icing (confectioner's) sugar off the cut-out pieces.

6 Place the roof pieces in position on the side of the cake, and the windows on the top, securing with a little apricot glaze or royal icing.

GHOSTS

7 For each of the three ghosts, roll a size A and a size C ball between the palms of your hands. Knead and roll the two balls together, mould into a ghostly shape and squash flat. Shape balls of black paste into flat oval shapes and press them on to the ghosts to represent eyes and mouths.

8 Place the ghosts in position on the house, securing with a little royal icing or apricot glaze.

FINISHING

9 To make the full moon, mould a piece of white sugarpaste into a size C ball (see page 12) and flatten it. Fix it on to the cake board with a little royal icing or apricot glaze.

10 Pipe white royal icing along some of the lines of the brickwork on the top and sides of the cake. Colour some royal icing green and use it to pipe grass on the board around the house and doorway, and ivy climbing up the walls of the house (see page 15). Trim the board with ribbon.

CIRCUS CLOWN

THIS HAPPY LITTLE CLOWN is very easy to make. You could even make two or three more clowns in different colours to keep him company on the cake!

You will need

- 1.5kg (3lb) white sugarpaste for cake and board
- red, yellow, orange, green, pink and black food colourings
- icing (confectioner's) sugar for dusting
- apricot glaze (see page 6)
- 28cm (11 inch) round cake board
- 20 x 15cm (8 x 6 inch) scalloped oval cake
- jam for filling
- filling cream (see page 6)
- crimper
- cocktail stick (toothpick)
- impressing tool
- sharp knife or scalpel
- green ribbon to trim cake
- 60g (2oz) royal icing (see page 6)
- 185g (6oz) sugarpaste for clown and juggling balls
- raw dried spaghetti
- paintbrush
- black icing pen
- small paper piping bag (see page 14)
- ribbon to trim board

Colour and Size Guide for the Clown and Juggling Balls

(see pages 5 and 12)

shoes (green)	2 x F
body (red)	A
arms (red)	2 x F
hands ('flesh')	2 x H
ruffle (yellow and green)	2 x G
head ('flesh')	D
nose (red)	J
balls (red)	5 x H
balls (yellow)	5 x H

☆ Remember! Roll and shape each ball of paste as you need it, not in advance.

PREPARING CAKE AND BOARD

1 Colour 315g (10oz) sugarpaste red, roll it out and use it to cover the cake board, following the instructions on page 9. Leave to set overnight.

2 Cut the cake horizontally in half and fill with jam and filling cream. Place the filled cake carefully in the centre of the paste-covered board.

3 Roll out 1kg (2lb) white sugarpaste and use it to cover the cake following the instructions on page 8. Using a crimper, crimp a decorative line around the cake about a quarter of the way up from the base.

4 Using a cocktail stick (toothpick) or the pointed end of an impressing tool, mark a hole above each point in the crimped pattern.

5 Colour the remaining white sugarpaste yellow and roll it out to about 2.5mm (⅛ inch) thick. Using a sharp knife or scalpel, cut out 20 yellow triangles of the size shown in the diagram below, and position them on the board around the cake.

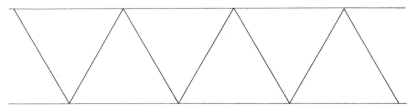

6 Attach a length of green ribbon around the cake, halfway up the sides, and secure with a dot of royal icing.

THE CLOWN

7 Following the colour and size guide on page 37, divide 185g (6oz) sugarpaste into rough portions and colour as required. Put in separate polythene bags.

8 Beginning with the clown's shoes, roll two size F balls of green sugarpaste and form them into elongated pear shapes. Flatten them slightly, and place them side by side on top of the cake.

9 Shape a red size A ball into a cone and place it on top of the clown's shoes for the body. Make a shallow cut in the middle of the front of the body from the bottom to about halfway up to represent the clown's coat.

10 For the arms, roll each ball into an elongated, curved teardrop shape, tapering at one end. With the pointed ends at the top, attach the arms to the clown's body. Push a piece of spaghetti down through the centre of the body and break it off about 8mm (⅓ inch) above the body.

11 For the clown's hands, roll each of the 'flesh'-coloured balls into a teardrop shape. Twist the pointed end of the impressing tool into the end of each of the clown's arms to make a hole. Place the pointed ends of the 'hands' into the holes, pressing in well.

12 For the ruffle around the clown's neck, roll a yellow size G ball into a thin round, and frill the edges by rolling with a cocktail stick (toothpick) or frilling tool (see page 11). (Alternatively, cut out a scalloped round of paste with a small carnation cutter.) Place the ruffle down over the spaghetti. Repeat to make a green ruffle using a second size G ball.

13 Roll a size D ball of 'flesh'-coloured sugarpaste as smooth as possible, and press it down on to the spaghetti protruding from the top of the body. Make a hole in the centre of the face with the pointed tool. Roll a size J ball of red paste for the nose, pinch one side into a point, and press it firmly into the hole in the face.

14 Mark the eyes with the tip of a cocktail stick (toothpick) dipped in black colouring, and paint on a huge smile with diluted colouring and a paintbrush or a black icing pen.

15 Colour some royal icing orange and use to pipe hair in tufts on either side of the clown's head, following the instructions on page 15.

FINISHING

16 Roll about ten size H red and yellow balls, and arrange around the clown on top of the cake and on the cake board. Trim the board with ribbon.

MR MOLE

THIS LITTLE MOLE bursting up through the soil will brighten up your party and make a lovely table centrepiece. If you like, you could make it a more creepy-crawly design by adding some worms and caterpillars or slugs and snails!

You will need

- 15cm (6 inch) square cake
- 25cm (10 inch) square cake board
- jam for filling
- filling cream (see page 6)
- 1.1kg (2lb 2oz) white sugarpaste
- orange, yellow, brown, green and black food colourings
- icing (confectioner's) sugar for dusting
- apricot glaze (see page 6)
- crimper
- 90g (3oz) royal icing (see page 6)
- 125g (4oz) soft dark brown sugar
- paintbrush
- 125g (4oz) black sugarpaste for Mr Mole
- impressing tool
- cocktail stick (toothpick)
- small paper piping bag (see page 14)
- ribbon to trim board

Size Guide for Mr Mole
(see page 12)

paws	2 x E
body	A + C (rolled together)
nose	J
eyes	2 x K

☆ Remember! Roll and shape each ball of paste as you need it, not in advance.

PREPARING CAKE AND BOARD

1 Place the cake on the cake board, positioning it at an angle and closer to one corner of the board. Cut the cake horizontally in half and fill with jam and filling cream.

2 Colour 875g (1¾lb) sugarpaste a sandy colour using orange, yellow and brown colouring. Roll it out and use it to cover the cake and board together, following the instructions on page 8. Trim off and reserve excess sugarpaste.

3 Using a crimper, mark a decorative zig-zag line all around the board about 1cm (½ inch) in from the edge.

4 Pile the reserved sugarpaste trimmings in a mound on the board at the front corner of the cake. Colour 60g (2oz) royal icing the same shade as the cake and board, and spread it roughly over the mound. Spread more royal icing down the front corner of the cake and on to the board.

5 Sprinkle brown sugar over the royal icing, pressing it on lightly before the icing sets. Sprinkle more sugar in a mound on top of the cake.

PEBBLES

6 Divide 60g (2oz) white sugarpaste in half and colour one half grey using black colouring. Add the white paste and knead together lightly to make a 'mottled' or marbled effect (see page 5). Roll the paste into different-sized pebbles. Scatter these around the cake and fix in position with a little royal icing or apricot glaze, if necessary.

TOADSTOOLS

7 For the stem of each toadstool, roll a sausage of white sugarpaste and press it against the side of the cake. Colour 60g (2oz) sugarpaste

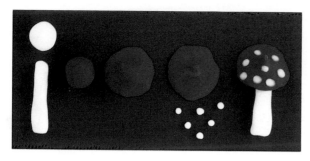

red (or use ready-coloured paste). For a large toadstool, mould a size D ball of red sugarpaste (size F for a small toadstool; see page 12). Pinch around the edge of the ball, stretching the paste out thinly around the edges, but leaving it thick in the centre. Pull the top centre up into a point.

8 Press tiny balls of white sugarpaste on to the surfaces of the red toadstool tops to make white spots. Place the red tops on top of the stems, leaning the toadstools against the sides of the cake so they don't topple over. (Pipe a little grass, as described on page 15, around the base of the toadstool to keep it in place, if necessary.)

Mr Mole

9 Beginning with the paws, roll two size E balls of black paste between the palms of your hands, mould each into a teardrop shape, and then squash them flat.

To splay out the feet, mark three deep indentations in the wide end of each paw with the pointed end of an impressing tool. Use the tip of a cocktail stick (toothpick) to mark a claw at the end of each 'toe'.

10 For Mr Mole's body, roll a size A and a size C ball of black paste, knead and roll them together, then shape into a cone. Bend the tip of the cone over to shape the nose. Push the base of the cone gently into the pile of sugar on top of the cake. Tuck the narrow end of one paw under the body, and position the other in the sugar slightly to one side of the body.

11 For the nose, make a hole in the tip of the

cone with the pointed tool. Form a size J ball of black paste into a teardrop shape and push the point into the hole. For the eyes, squash two tiny balls of black paste flat and press them on to the mole's face. Mark two indentations for the ears with the ball end of the impressing tool.

Finishing

12 Scratch the body of the mole with the tip of a cocktail stick (toothpick) to give the impression of fur. Colour the remaining royal icing green and use to pipe grass around the toadstools and pebbles, and on the top of the cake (see page 15). Trim the board with ribbon.

Tip

☆ To make Mr Mole's nose and eyes bright, brush them with a little confectioner's varnish. Give him a sparkle in his eye with tiny dots of white royal icing.

TIGER, TIGER

THIS JUNGLE SCENE will appeal to all! For greater effect, add more tigers peering through the grass on the sides of the cake.

You will need

- 1.9kg (3lb 14oz) white sugarpaste
- green, brown, blue, pink, black and orange food colouring
- icing (confectioner's) sugar for dusting
- 33cm (13 inch) square cake board
- apricot glaze (see page 6)
- 20cm (8 inch) square cake, 10cm (4 inches) deep
- jam for filling
- filling cream (see page 6)
- crimper
- cocktail stick (toothpick)
- impressing tool
- 60g (2oz) royal icing (optional), see page 6
- 90g (3oz) sugarpaste for tiger
- paintbrush (optional)
- black icing pen (optional)
- ribbon to trim board

remove shaded area

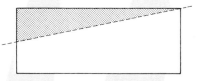

PREPARING CAKE AND BOARD

1 Colour 440g (14oz) sugarpaste dark green, roll it out and use it to cover the cake board, following the instructions on page 9. Leave to set overnight.

2 To make this design stand out more clearly, the cake is cut to a steep slope. Using a large, sharp, serrated knife, and starting at one top edge, cut through the cake at an angle so your knife emerges halfway down the opposite side (see diagram). Remove the wedge of sponge from the top of the cake.

3 Cut the remaining cake horizontally in half and fill with jam and filling cream. Carefully place the cake on the covered board.

4 Colour 1.25kg (2½lb) sugarpaste pale green, roll it out and use it to cover the cake following the instructions on page 8. Using a crimper, crimp a decorative border in the sugarpaste around the top edge of the cake.

GRASS

5 Divide another 185g (6oz) sugarpaste in half and colour in two different shades of green, making sure the colours complement those already used on cake and board. Roll out both pieces thinly.

6 Trace the grass outlines on page 63 on to greaseproof or non-stick paper, cut them out and use them as templates to cut out 30 or 40 different-sized pieces, using both shades of green sug-

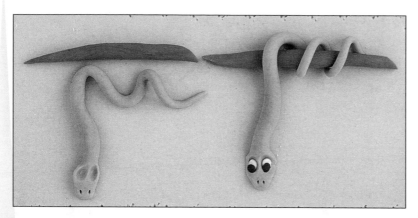

arpaste. Leave these to dry, lying some of them flat and curving others sideways so they harden in a curved shape.

TREE AND SNAKE

7 Colour a small amount of sugarpaste a mid-brown colour and shape it into a size B ball (see page 12). Roll it into a long tapering sausage shape about 15cm (6 inches) long and position it on the side of the cake, bending it over on to the top of the cake.

8 Roll some more small, thin, tapered sausages of brown paste and attach to either side of the tree trunk for branches. Smooth over joins with your fingers.

9 For the snake, colour a small amount of sugarpaste pale mauve with blue and pink colouring, and shape into a size D ball (see page 12). Roll into a sausage 13cm (5 inches) long, tapering one end to a point. Flatten the other end by pinching it between your fingers.

10 Make another 'branch' of brown paste and wrap the snake around it, leaving the snake's head and some of its body free. Position on the cake so the snake appears to be dangling from the branch.

11 Mark two tiny holes with a cocktail stick (toothpick) for the snake's nostrils, and make two eye indentations with the pointed end of an impressing tool. Squash two small balls of white sugarpaste into flat oval shapes, and squash a tiny ball of black paste on to one end of each oval. Press the eyes gently into the indentations on each side of the snake's head.

ATTACHING THE GRASS

12 Stick blades of grass on to the cake with a little royal icing or apricot glaze. Use the longer blades to the left and right on top of the cake, with shorter blades in the centre. Attach grass around the sides and back of the cake as well. Reserve seven or eight short blades of grass for placing over the tiger.

THE TIGER

13 Following the guide on page 43, divide 90g (3oz) sugarpaste into roughly the proportions required for each colour, and colour them as indicated. Place in separate polythene bags.

14 Beginning with the tiger's legs, roll a size D ball of paste between the palms of your hands and shape it into a sausage 10cm (4 inches) long. Cut it into four equal sections. Place one front leg and one back leg in position on the cake and squash flat.

15 For the tiger's body, form a size B ball into a short, fat sausage shape,

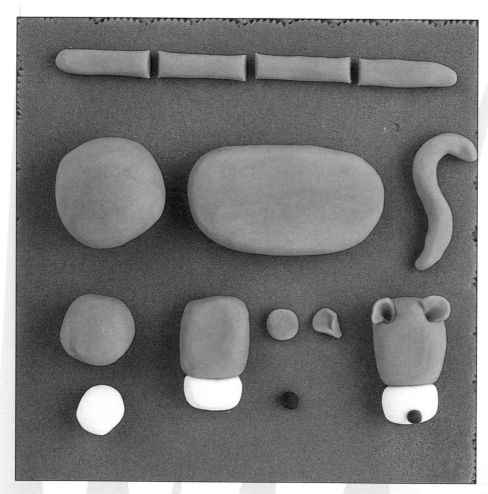

18 For the tiger's ears, use a pointed tool to make two 5mm (¼ inch) holes in the top of the tiger's head. Squash two size H balls flat and pinch one side of each into a point, curling the sides of the pieces towards the centre slightly to give them an ear-like shape. Place the pointed ends of the ears into the holes in the head, pushing them in with a pointed tool.

Finishing

19 Paint on the tiger's markings and eyes using a fine paintbrush and diluted black food colouring or a black icing pen. Leave to dry completely.

20 Arrange the reserved pieces of grass on top of the tiger, and stick in place with a little royal icing or apricot glaze. Scratch marks on the tree trunk with a cocktail stick (toothpick). Make another snake for the board, if you wish. Trim the board with ribbon.

place it on the cake at the top of the legs and squash flat. Stick the other two legs on to the body, bending them both forwards slightly.

16 For the tiger's tail, roll a size F ball until it is 5cm (2 inches) long, and place it at the end of the body, curling it around the grass. Press it into place, flattening it slightly.

17 Squash a size D ball of paste into a rectangular shape for the head and place it at the end of the body. Press the white muzzle firmly into place on the lower end of the head. Use a pointed tool to make a hole in the end of the nose. Shape a size J ball of black paste into a teardrop shape and press the pointed end into the hole, pushing it in firmly.

FROG POND

THESE HAPPY GREEN FROGS look about to hop into the water, or off the cake! Add as many little frogs around the cake board as you like.

You will need

- 20cm (8 inch) oval cake
- 25cm (10 inch) oval cake board
- jam for filling
- filling cream (see page 6)
- 1.7kg (3lb 6oz) white sugarpaste
- green, black and turquoise food colourings
- icing (confectioner's) sugar for dusting
- apricot glaze (see page 6)
- impressing tool
- cocktail stick (toothpick)
- paintbrush
- clear piping gel
- orange paper ribbon
- 125g (4oz) sugarpaste for frogs
- ribbon to trim board

Size Guide for Frogs
(see page 12)

	large	small
body and head (dark green)	A	B
eyes (white)	H	I
pupils (black)	I	J
legs (dark green)	2 x D	2 x E

☆ Remember! Roll and shape each ball of paste as you need it, not in advance.

PREPARING CAKE AND BOARD

1 Place the cake on the cake board, positioning it to one side of the board. Cut the cake horizontally in half and fill with jam and filling cream.

2 Colour 1.5kg (3lb) sugarpaste very pale green, roll it out and use it to coat the cake and board together, following the instructions on page 8. Using the end of an impressing tool, mark a pattern around the edge of the board. Mark scratches with a cocktail stick (toothpick) in places in the sugarpaste on the sides of the cake to give a textured effect.

PEBBLES

3 Divide 125g (4oz) sugarpaste in two and colour one half dark grey with black food colouring. Knead together lightly with the other half of the paste until marbled grey in colour. Shape the paste into irregular-shaped 'pebbles' of different sizes.

PONDS

4 Arrange some pebbles in an oval on the top of the

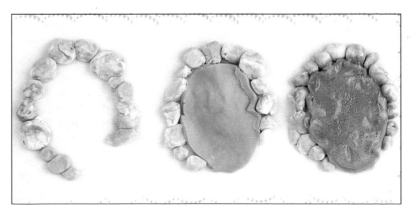

cake for the edge of the pond. Build another layer of pebbles on top of the first. Form another smaller pond on the cake board. Scratch the surface of some of the pebbles with the pointed end of the impressing tool.

5 Divide 60g (2oz) sugarpaste in half and colour one half green and the other turquoise. Knead the two pieces together lightly to create a marbled green/turquoise effect. Roll out the paste and cut a piece large enough to fit into the base of the pond. Reserve the trimmings. Brush the underside of the paste with apricot glaze and fit the piece inside the oval of pebbles on top of the cake. Spoon clear piping gel on top, filling the pond.

6 Knead and roll out the turquoise/green trimmings and use to make the small pond on the board. Cover with a little piping gel as for the top pond. Cut out some small fish shapes from bright orange paper ribbon and push them down into the 'water' in both ponds. (Do not use orange sugarpaste as the colour will run.)

FROGS

7 Following the guide on page 47, divide 125g (4oz)

sugarpaste into roughly the proportions required for each colour, and colour as indicated. Place in separate polythene bags. Make one large and one small frog; both are made in the same way.

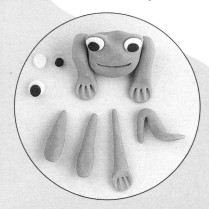

8 Roll a large ball of dark green paste between the palms of your hands to make the frog's body and head. Pinch the top of the ball in two places between your thumb and forefinger, pulling the paste upwards to form the eyes. Press the paste down with your finger on the top of the ball between the eyes, as illustrated in the diagram.

9 For the eyes, squash the balls of paste into white ovals. For the pupils, press a tiny black ball of paste on to one end of each oval. Position the eyes on the frog, pressing to stick and using a little apricot glaze if necessary.

10 For the frog's legs, roll each ball of paste into a long teardrop shape. Flatten the wide end and mark three indentations in it with the pointed end of an impressing tool. Bend over the pointed end of the paste, and bend up the foot so that it will sit flat on the cake surface. Place one leg on either side of the body. Press the edge of a teaspoon into the frog's face, giving it a big smile. Leave to harden.

FINISHING

11 Place the frogs on the cake and board, securing with a little apricot glaze. Trim the board with ribbon.

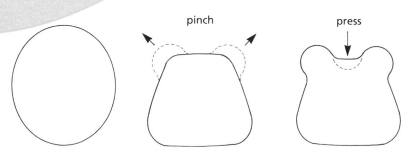

pinch

press

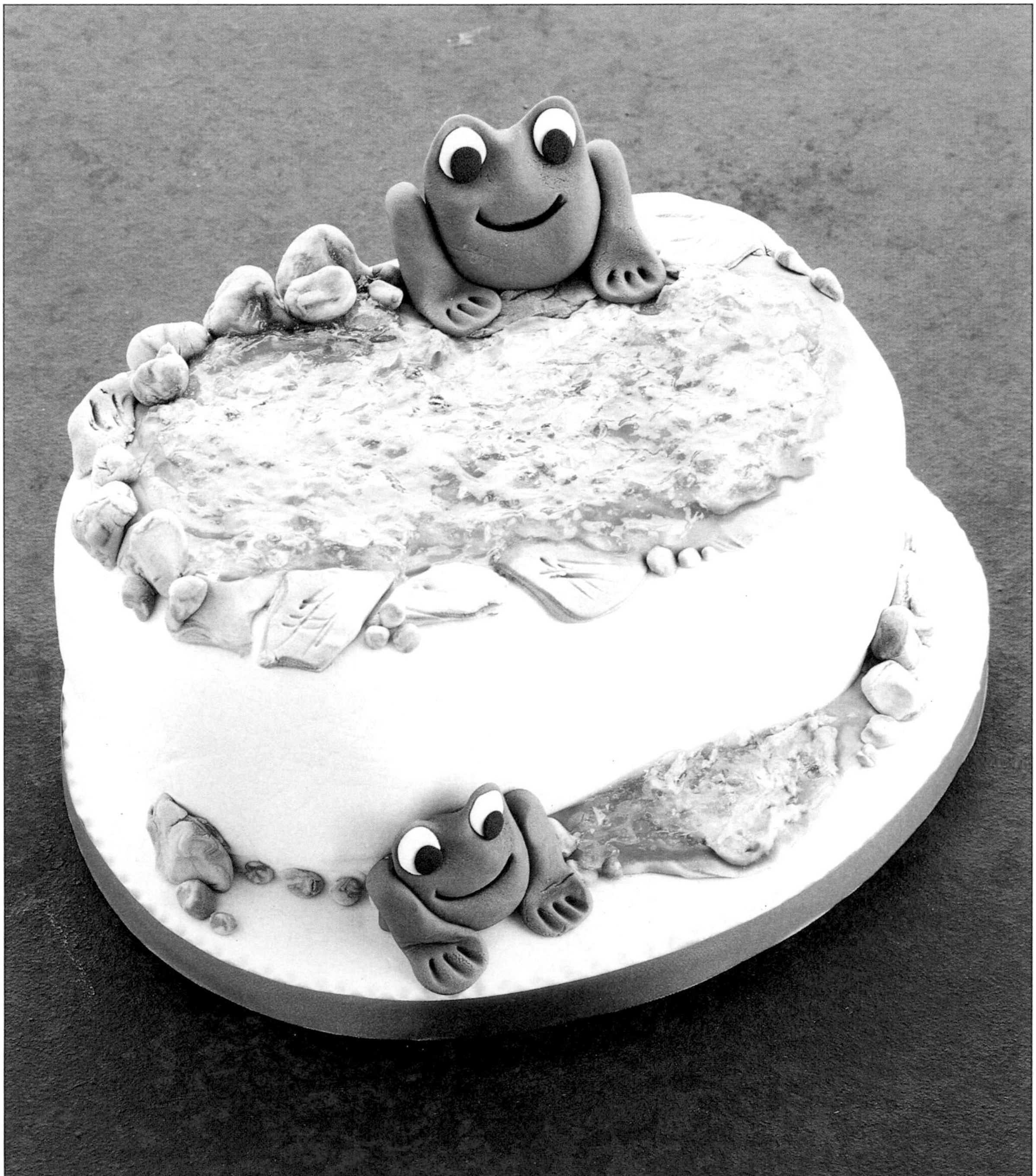

WHAT A SAVE!

IF THERE'S A FOOTBALL FAN in your family, you'll know how popular this cake will be, but make sure the goalie is dressed in the right colours!

You will need

- 20 x 25cm (8 x 10 inch) scalloped oval cake
- 30cm (12 inch) round cake board
- jam for filling
- filling cream (see page 6)
- 1.6kg (3¼lb) white sugarpaste
- green, red, pink, yellow and black food colourings
- icing (confectioner's) sugar for dusting
- apricot glaze (see page 6)
- crimper
- 60g (2oz) royal icing (see page 6)
- 45g (1½oz) sugarpaste for the goalie
- paintbrush
- impressing tool
- cocktail stick (toothpick)
- 3 small paper piping bags (see page 14)
- 30g (1oz) black sugarpaste
- sharp knife or scalpel
- no. 1 piping tube (tip)
- ribbon to trim board

PREPARING CAKE AND BOARD

1 Place the cake on the cake board. Cut the cake horizontally in half and fill with jam and filling cream.

2 Colour 1.5kg (3lb) sugarpaste grass green, roll it

Colour and Size Guide for the Goalie
(see pages 5 and 12)

shorts (white)	F
body (red)	B
neck ('flesh')	G
arms (red)	D
hands ('flesh')	2 x G
head ('flesh')	D
nose ('flesh')	J

☆ Remember! Roll and shape each ball of paste as you need it, not in advance.

out and use it to cover the cake and board together, following the instructions on page 8. Use a crimper to mark decorative borders in the sugarpaste around the edge of the cake and the board. Leave to harden.

GOAL POSTS

3 Roll out 30g (1oz) white sugarpaste to 25cm (10 inches) long and trim it to a 5mm (¼ inch) wide strip. Cut the strip into three pieces, one 10cm (4 inches) long (for the top bar) and two 7.5cm (3 inches) long (for the uprights). Stick these on the cake with a little green royal icing (see the positioning guide on page 64).

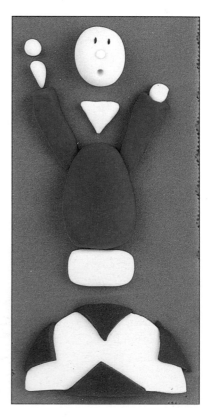

GOALIE

4 Following the guide on page 50, divide 45g (1½ oz) sugarpaste into roughly the proportions required for each colour, and colour as indicated. Place the different-coloured portions of sugarpaste in separate polythene bags.

5 Begin by making the goalie's shorts. Roll a size F ball of white paste between the palms of your hands, and shape it into a squashed rectangle. Press it on to the cake (approximately in the centre). Form a size B ball of red paste into a rounded cone shape for the goalie's body, and squash it flat. Position it above and slightly overlapping the shorts. Shape a size G ball of 'flesh'-coloured paste into a triangular shape for the goalie's neck, and press it on to the top of the body.

6 For the arms, roll a size D ball of red paste into a sausage 7.5cm (3 inches) long. Cut this in half and place one on either side of the body, attaching the cut end of each arm to the 'shoulders' and positioning them so the goalie has his arms up. Use a tiny amount of red royal icing to stick the arms to the body and to the top of the cake.

7 Form two balls of paste for the hands into teardrop shapes. Push the pointed end of an impressing tool into the end of each arm to make a hole, and push the pointed ends of the hands into them.

8 To make the goalie's head, form a size D ball of 'flesh'-coloured paste and make it as smooth as possible. Place it at the top of the body, securing with a little royal icing. Make a hole with a pointed tool in the centre of the face. Roll a ball of paste for the nose, form it into a teardrop shape, and push it into the hole, pressing it in well. Mark the eyes with the tip of a cocktail stick (toothpick) dipped in black food colouring, and either paint on a smile or mark a round mouth with a pointed tool. Pipe some hair on the goalie's head using yellow royal icing in a small paper piping bag (see page 15).

FOOTBALL

9 Form 75g (2½oz) white sugarpaste into a ball. Squash the ball flat into a circle about 8.5cm (3½ inches) in diameter. Place on the cake, covering most of the goalie's shorts, and stick with a little royal icing. Use the diagram on page 64 as a positioning guide.

10 Trace the triangle and pentagon outlines on page 64 on to greaseproof or non-stick paper and cut them out. Roll out 30g (1oz) black sugarpaste and use the templates and a sharp knife or scalpel to cut out five triangles and one pentagon. Using royal icing, stick the triangles around the edge of the football and the pentagon in the centre.

FINISHING

11 Using white royal icing in a paper piping bag (see page 14) fitted with a no. 1 tube (tip), pipe the lines of the goal net on to the cake. Alternatively, mark the lines in the sugarpaste with a cocktail stick (toothpick).

12 Pipe patches of grass at the bottom of the goal posts and around the sides of the cake (see page 15). Scratch a few lines across the surface of the cake to add some texture. Trim the cake board with ribbon.

Tip

☆ Use the diagram on page 64 to help position the goal and ball on the top of the cake.

ONE IN A BED

'THERE WERE TEN IN THE BED, and the little one said . . .' Here is the little one, sleeping soundly! Put as many children in the bed as you like, depending on the age of the birthday boy or girl.

You will need

- 20cm (8 inch) oval cake
- 25cm (10 inch) round cake board
- jam for filling
- filling cream (see page 6)
- 1.6kg (3¼lb) white sugarpaste
- icing (confectioner's) sugar for dusting
- apricot glaze (see page 6)
- blue, black, brown, pink and yellow food colourings
- crimper
- ribbon to trim cake
- 60g (2oz) royal icing (see page 6)
- 60g (2oz) sugarpaste for the 'little one'
- cocktail stick (toothpick)
- impressing tool
- paintbrush
- small paper piping bag (see page 14)
- 60g (2oz) sugarpaste for the toy hippo
- no.1 piping tube (tip)
- ribbon to trim board

PREPARING CAKE AND BOARD

1 Position the cake centrally on the cake board. Carefully cut the cake horizontally in half and fill with jam and filling cream.

Size Guide for the 'Little One' and Hippo

(see page 12)

'Little One'		Hippo	
body	C	body	C
head	D	front legs	2 x F
nose	K	back legs	2 x F
		head	E
		ears	2 x I

☆ Remember! Roll and shape each ball of paste as you need it, not in advance.

2 Roll out 1.25kg (2½lb) white sugarpaste and use to cover the cake and board together, following the instructions on page 8.

3 Colour 220g (7oz) sugarpaste blue and divide in half. Roll one half into a long sausage and place it on the board around the base of the cake. Make the join as smooth as possible and at the back of the cake. Use a crimper to mark a zig-zag pattern in the roll of paste.

Attach a length of ribbon around the cake above the roll of paste, securing with a dot of royal icing. Crimp another zig-zag border around the sides of the cake, just above the ribbon.

PILLOWS

4 Roll 15g (½oz) white sugarpaste into a sausage 7.5cm (3 inches) long and place on top of the cake about 1cm (½ inch) in from one long edge. Secure with a little royal icing or apricot glaze and press an indentation in the top of the pillow

press with thumb

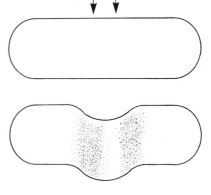

with your thumb to accommodate the head.

5 Make a similar, smaller pillow for the toy hippo, and place it on the cake board.

BEDSPREAD

6 Colour the 60g (2oz) sugarpaste for the little one 'flesh'-coloured (see page 5). Place in a polythene bag. To make a bump in the bed for the little one's body, roll some of the 'flesh'-coloured sugarpaste into a size C ball between the palms of your hands. Shape it into an oval and place it on top of the cake about 2.5cm (1 inch) below the pillow.

7 Roll out the remaining blue sugarpaste until it is about 5mm (¼ inch) thick. Cut out a 15 x 23cm (6 x 9 inch) oval and frill the edges (see page 11).

8 Spread a small amount of filling cream or apricot glaze on the top of the cake and stick the bedspread in place, folding back the edge to reveal the pillow.

LITTLE ONE

9 Using the remaining 'flesh'-coloured paste, make the head of the small person in bed. Roll a size D

ball of paste until it is as smooth as possible, and make a small hole in the centre with the pointed end of an impressing tool. Place the head on the pillow, resting it in the hollow already formed. For the nose, pinch one side of a size K ball into a point and place it in the hole in the face. Press in well.

10 For the mouth, either make a hole with a pointed tool, or paint on a smile with a paintbrush and diluted black colouring. Mark the eyes with the tip of a cocktail stick (toothpick) dipped in black colouring, or paint on closed eyes and lashes with a paintbrush. Pipe hair on to the head using brown royal icing (see page 15).

TOY HIPPO

11 Colour 60g (2oz) sugarpaste grey with a little black colouring, and put in a polythene bag. For the

body, roll a size C ball of paste between the palms of your hands, and shape it into an oval. Place it on the cake board, leaning against the pillow. Mark a tummy button with the point of a cocktail stick (toothpick). Form size F balls for the back legs into teardrop shapes. Pinch the fat end of each to form a foot. Attach the thinner ends of the legs to the body (using a little apricot glaze, if necessary). Make the front legs in the same way and attach to the top of the body.

12 For the head, mould a size E ball into a pear shape and place it on top of the body, covering the tops of the arms with the wider end of the pear shape. Mark two big nostrils in the hippo's nose with a pointed tool.

13 Make two smaller holes in the top of the hippo's head. Squash flat two size I balls for the ears and

pinch one side of each to a point, curling the sides inwards to make ear shapes. Press the points of the ears into the holes in the hippo's head with a pointed tool. Add eyes as for the little one (see step 10, above).

FINISHING

14 Roll out some white sugarpaste and cut out a crescent moon shape (using the outline on page 63 to make a template). Stick on to the bedspread with a little royal icing or apricot glaze,

and use a cocktail stick (toothpick) to mark features. Pipe stars on the bedspread with white royal icing in a bag fitted with a no. 1 tube (tip), or cut out sugarpaste stars and stick on with icing. Trim the cake board with ribbon.

THE MOUSE'S TAIL

THE OPEN-BOOK THEME can be used over and over again simply by changing the colours, the message and the animals.

You will need

- 500g (1lb) ivory sugarpaste
- icing (confectioner's) sugar for dusting
- 40cm (16 inch) square cake board
- apricot glaze (see page 6)
- 23 x 30cm (9 x 12 inch) rectangular cake
- jam for filling
- filling cream (see page 6)
- 1.9kg (3¾lb) deep cream sugarpaste
- 30g (1oz) royal icing (see page 6)
- brown, black, pink and green food colourings
- paintbrush
- cocktail stick (toothpick)
- brown icing pen
- 250g (8oz) sugarpaste for mice
- impressing tool
- white flower stamens
- silk or sugar leaves (see page 59)
- small paper piping bag (see page 14)
- ribbon to trim board

Colour and Size Guide for Mice
(see pages 5 and 12)

	large	medium	small
body (grey)	A + B	A	C
ears (grey)	2 x F	2 x G	2 x H
inner ears (pink)	2 x H	2 x I	2 x J
nose (black)	J	K	K
tail (grey)	E	F	G

☆ Remember! Roll and shape each ball of paste as you need it, not in advance.

PREPARING CAKE AND BOARD

1 Roll out the ivory sugarpaste and use to cover the cake board, following the instructions on page 9. Use a teaspoon handle to mark a border around the edge. Leave to harden overnight.

2 Cut the cake horizontally in half and fill with jam and filling cream. Slope the sides of the cake by carving wedges off the top edges (see diagram). Place the cake on the covered board and spread it all over with filling cream.

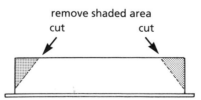

remove shaded area
cut   cut

3 Roll out 1.5kg (3lb) deep cream sugarpaste and use to cover the cake following the instructions on page 8. Mark lines with the back of a knife

along the sloping sides of the cake to represent pages.

TOP PAGE

4 Roll out another 185g (6oz) cream sugarpaste and cut a piece the size of the top of the cake. Smear a little royal icing on the top of the cake and stick the piece of sugarpaste in position. Nudge the edges of the top page upwards, especially at the corners.

BACK COVER

5 Colour 185g (6oz) cream sugarpaste brown and roll out to a rectangle measuring

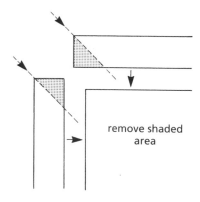

remove shaded area

13 x 30cm (5 x 12 inches). Cut two 30cm (12 inch) strips 2.5cm (1 inch) wide, and stick one on the cake board along the base of each long side of the cake. Cut two more strips measuring 2.5 x 23cm (1 x 9 inches) and place along the shorter sides. Cut the ends of the strips at an angle so they form neat joins at the corners (see diagram). Pinch the corners into points.

6 Cut a final strip of brown paste for the bookmark. Make several cuts in each end to make 'tassels'. Fix the bookmark across the centre of the cake. Using a cocktail stick (toothpick), scratch lines in all the brown sugarpaste to give a 'worn leather' look.

LETTERING

7 Roll trimmings of brown sugarpaste into three sausage shapes about 2.5cm (1 inch) long. Flatten slightly and place in position on the cake to form the upright parts of the capital letters (T, M and T). For extra guidance when positioning, trace the outline of the lettering on page 63 on to a piece of greaseproof or non-stick paper the size of the top of the cake. Lay it on top of the cake, and use a cocktail stick to mark the surface of the cake through the paper.

8 Using a brown icing pen, complete the lettering on the cake. Add a decorative motif beneath and in the top right-hand corner (copying the design on page 63, if required). Mark a border all around the edges and mark lines of 'print' on the right-hand page.

MICE

9 Colour about 15g (½oz) sugarpaste pink and the remainder grey. Put in separate polythene bags. Make one large, three medium and two small mice; all are made in the same way, following the size guide on page 56.

10 For the body, roll a ball of grey paste between the palms of your hands, and form it into a teardrop shape. Place on the cake or board. Gently nudge the pointed end upwards to form the nose. Using the pointed end of an impressing tool, make two holes in the top of the head for ears. Make a small hole in the tip of the nose.

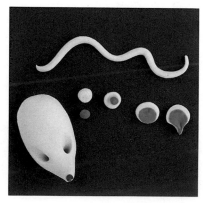

Colouring Tip

☆ If you cannot buy ready-coloured deep cream sugarpaste, colour white sugarpaste with a tiny amount of orange food colouring.

11 For the ears, roll balls of pink and grey paste and squash them flat. Place the pink inner ear piece on top of the grey piece and press well together. Pinch one side of each into a point and push into the holes in the head. Press them in well, using the pointed tool.

12 Colour a tiny amount of the grey paste black, and roll it into a small ball for the nose. Shape it into a teardrop shape, place the point in the hole in the mouse's nose, and press in well. Mark the eyes with the point of a cocktail stick dipped in black colouring.

13 The whiskers are made from white flower stamens. Cut the ends off the stamens and push them into the paste on either side of the mouse's nose. Mark lines of 'fur' on the mouse's body with the tip of a cocktail stick (toothpick).

14 For the mouse's tail, roll the ball of paste into a long sausage, rolling one end to a fine point. Tuck the blunt end under the back of the mouse's body and arrange the tail on the cake or board, securing it in position with a little royal icing, if necessary.

LEAVES

15 To make sugar leaves, colour 60g (2oz) sugarpaste pale green and roll it out to about 2.5mm (⅛ inch) thick. Cut out leaves using a rose leaf cutter, and mark veins with a knife or leaf veiner. Roll gently around the

Tip

☆ Flower stamens are available from specialist cake-decorating and sugarcraft shops.

edges of each leaf with the rounded end of an impressing tool to curl the edges slightly. Push some leaves on to wires. Leave to dry over a small rolling pin or similar curved shape so the leaves set in a natural shape. When dry, dust with dark green dusting powder.

FINISHING

16 Place the leaves on the cake and board in a 'tumbling' arrangement, securing them with a little royal icing. Wired leaves can be arranged in sprays.

17 Colour a little royal icing green and pipe decorative details on and around the sugarpaste parts of the lettering (see page 15 for piping instructions). Finish the design around the top of the cake. Trim the board with ribbon.

BALLOONS AND ELEPHANTS

BALLOONS AND STREAMERS help make any party go with a bang! The little elephants will appeal to everyone; if you have time, why not make enough for each party guest to take one home?

You will need

- 1.9kg (3¾lb) white sugarpaste
- icing (confectioner's) sugar for dusting
- 40cm (16 inch) round cake board
- apricot glaze (see page 6)
- crimper
- 2 cakes baked in 1.25 litre (2 pint/5 cup) pudding basins and measuring 15cm/6 inches at their widest and 7.5cm/3 inches high
- jam for filling
- filling cream (see page 6)
- blue, turquoise, pink and black food colourings
- Swiss roll (jelly roll)
- paintbrush
- 345g (11oz) sugarpaste for elephants
- impressing tool
- cocktail stick (toothpick)
- liquorice 'bootlaces' (optional)
- black icing pen (optional)
- paper ribbon for streamers
- ribbon to trim board

Size Guide for Elephants
(see page 12)

	large	small
body	A + B (rolled together)	B
feet	2 x E	2 x G
front legs	2 x D	2 x F
head and trunk	A	D
ears	2 x D	2 x F

☆ Remember! Roll and shape each ball of paste as you need it, not in advance.

PREPARING CAKES AND BOARD

1 Roll out 750g (1½lb) white sugarpaste and use it to cover the cake board, following the instructions on page 9. Using a crimper, mark a decorative pattern around the edge of the board. Leave to harden overnight.

2 Cut each of the two pudding basin cakes horizontally in half and fill with jam and filling cream.

BALLOONS

3 Colour three 315g (10oz) batches of sugarpaste blue, pale blue and turquoise, roll them out and use to cover the two sponges and the Swiss roll (jelly roll), trimming the paste to leave a little excess at the base of each cake. Reserve the trimmings.

Place the cakes on the covered board, tucking the spare sugarpaste in underneath each one.

4 Roll the different-coloured trimmings of paste into three separate size E balls (see page 12). Pull each one into a teardrop shape 7.5cm (3 inches) long. Bend the pointed end down and twist it round the fatter part of the teardrop, flattening it slightly to make it look like the knot in the neck of a balloon. Stick the knots to the ends of the balloons with a little apricot glaze.

ELEPHANTS

5 Colour 155g (5oz) sugarpaste pink and the remainder grey. Place in separate polythene bags. Make one large grey elephant, and three pink and one grey small elephants. All the elephants are made in the same way.

6 Begin by making the body. Roll a ball of paste between the palms of your hands and form it into an oval shape. Place it on the board, resting against a balloon. Make two round balls for the feet and press them on to the base of the body, squashing them flat. Mark three 'toe nails' with the pointed end of an impressing tool, and use the ball end of the tool to mark an indentation in the sole of each foot.

7 For the elephant's front legs, form each ball of paste into a long teardrop shape, and attach them, thin end uppermost, to the top of the body. (Use a tiny amount of apricot glaze to stick the pieces of sugarpaste together if necessary.)

8 The elephant's head and trunk are made by moulding the ball of paste into a pear shape and elongating the thinner end until it is long enough to form a trunk. Push the pointed tool into the end of the trunk to make a big hole. Mark horizontal lines on the trunk with the back of a knife, to give a realistic appearance.

9 For the ears, squash the two balls of paste flat and pinch one side of each to a point, curling the sides inwards slightly to make ear shapes. Make a 5mm (¼ inch) hole in each side of the elephant's head and place the points of the ears in them. Press the ears in well, using the pointed tool. Mark two eyes with the point of a cocktail stick (toothpick).

10 Place the elephant's head on top of the body, covering the tops of the front legs. Secure with a little apricot glaze, if necessary. Gently nudge the tip of the elephant's trunk upwards.

FINISHING

11 Roll the remaining white sugarpaste into three size C balls (see page 12). Roll each one into a long sausage, shape them into numerals, and gently squash on to the balloons.

12 The black strings of the balloons can be made from liquorice 'bootlaces' or painted on to the cake board with diluted black colouring and a paintbrush, or with a black icing pen. Arrange streamers made from curls of paper ribbon on and around the cakes, and trim the board with ribbon.

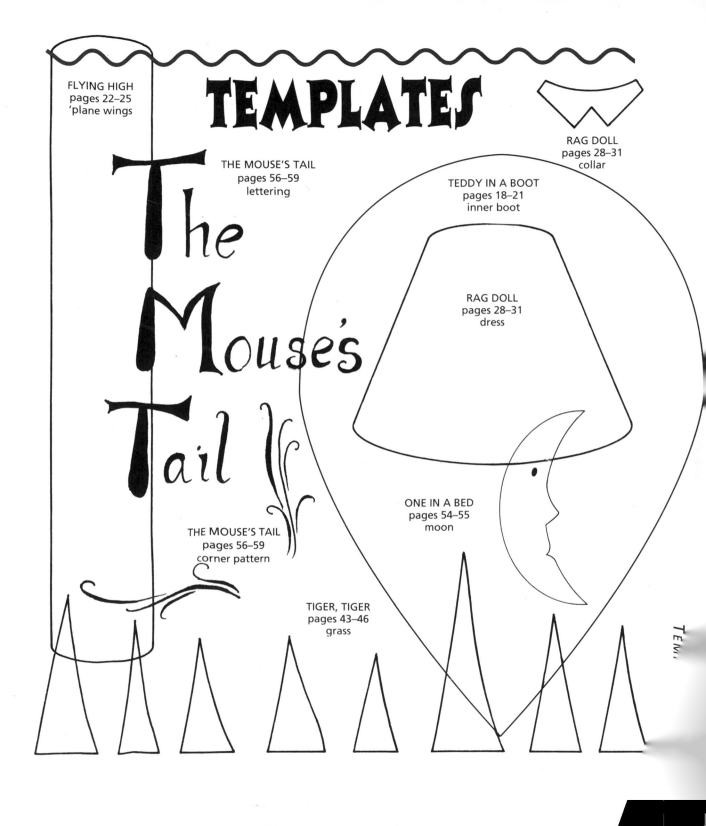

TEMPLATES

FLYING HIGH
pages 22–25
'plane wings

RAG DOLL
pages 28–31
collar

THE MOUSE'S TAIL
pages 56–59
lettering

TEDDY IN A BOOT
pages 18–21
inner boot

RAG DOLL
pages 28–31
dress

THE MOUSE'S TAIL
pages 56–59
corner pattern

ONE IN A BED
pages 54–55
moon

TIGER, TIGER
pages 43–46
grass

The Mouse's Tail

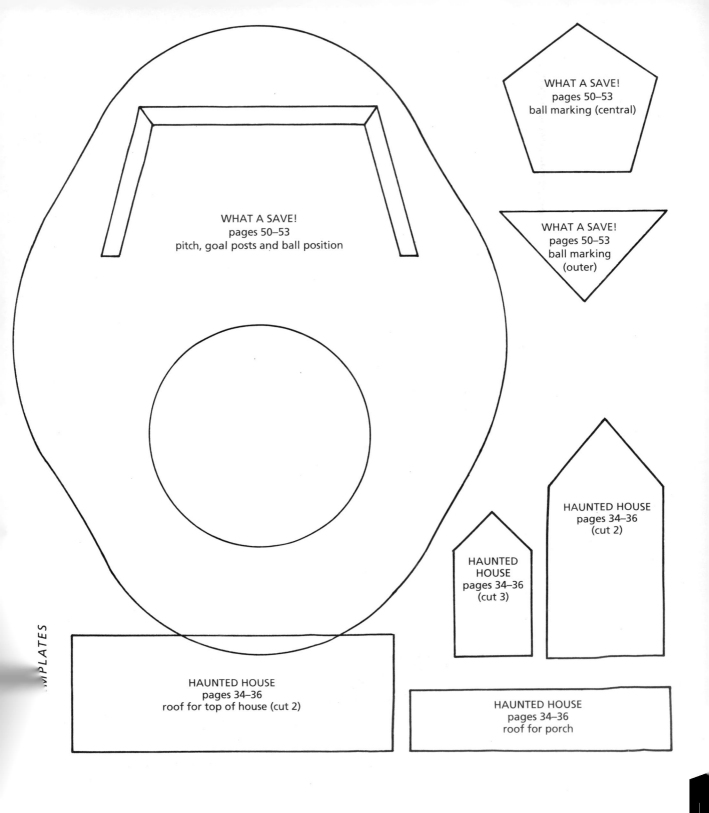

WHAT A SAVE!
pages 50–53
ball marking (central)

WHAT A SAVE!
pages 50–53
ball marking
(outer)

WHAT A SAVE!
pages 50–53
pitch, goal posts and ball position

HAUNTED HOUSE
pages 34–36
(cut 2)

HAUNTED
HOUSE
pages 34–36
(cut 3)

HAUNTED HOUSE
pages 34–36
roof for top of house (cut 2)

HAUNTED HOUSE
pages 34–36
roof for porch